D1176404

ELWOOD D. BAUMANN

BIGFOOT

America's Abominable Snowman

Published by
Dell Publishing Co., Inc.
1 Dag Hammarskjold Plaza
New York, New York 10017

To Tim and Mark Harder,
who helped me get started on—
BIGFOOT: America's Abominable Snowman

1

It was early on the morning of August 27, 1958, when Jerry Crew walked over to his bulldozer to begin his day's work. Suddenly he stopped and stared. A circle of enormous footprints went round and round his machine.

Crew scratched his head in amazement. No man on earth could have feet that size, he told himself. Besides, nobody lived in this huge, heavily forested wilderness in northern California. The area in which he was working covered seventeen thousand square miles of mountainous terrain that had never been explored. Except for the road gang, the country was completely uninhabited. Nothing there had changed for many thousands of years.

The first thought that came to Crew's mind was that someone was playing a prank on him. That idea, though, was quickly discarded. The men were simply too tired after a day in the woods to spend hours on a foolish trick. No, it wasn't a prank. Some creature had made the giant footprints—but what kind of creature?

When Crew followed the tracks, he found that the strides were twice as long as his own. Only by stretching his legs as far as possible could he reach from one print to another. Even more surprising was the fact that the unexplained footprints were pressed deeply into the floor of the forest. The bulldozer operator weighed about 165 pounds and his tracks were barely visible. This meant, then, that the creature who had made the tracks must have been several times heavier than a man of average weight.

It was a simple matter for Crew to follow the course the creature had taken. The tracks came almost straight down an incline of about seventy-five degrees. After circling the bulldozer a number of times, they continued along the newly built dirt road and finally turned off down an even steeper incline. The steep slopes and tangled underbrush were no problem at all for the visitor. It apparently walked through the most difficult terrain with no more effort than it takes a man to stroll down a sidewalk.

After investigating the tracks thoroughly, Crew drove to the camp at Bluff Creek and asked some of the other men to come up and have a look. They were as amazed as Jerry Crew had been. One of the men had a tape measure and found that the prints were sixteen inches long and seven inches wide. "No wonder the guy has to run around in his bare feet," he stated. "There's not a place in the world where they sell shoes big enough to fit feet that size."

All of the men agreed that the tracks could not have been made by a bear or any other kind of animal. Many of the prints clearly showed the heel, the ball of the foot, and five toes. Coming down the steep bank, the creature had dug in with its heels to get a more secure footing, which is exactly the way a man comes down a steep incline.

But what sort of a man could it possibly have been? they asked one another. It walked with five-foot strides and the depth of the prints in the soil indicated a weight of perhaps seven hundred fifty or eight hundred pounds.

2

Nearly a full month passed before the creature again appeared on the scene. After visiting the bulldozer, it walked down the road, had a drink from a spring, and once more disappeared into the forest. It came back on October 2, and on the next three mornings its tracks were found on the dirt road and around the machinery. On two occasions, a high-pitched whistling wail shattered the silence of the wilderness night.

The men on the road gang were understandably nervous. They lived in a remote camp in the uttermost back of nowhere. Civilization was many miles away over a tortuous mountain track. A heavy rainfall or a landslide could isolate them completely for days at a time.

"I don't like it one bit," one of the men finally admitted. "We've got this Giant Wild Man hanging around up here and there's nothing we can do about it. How do we know that the thing isn't going to come into camp and tear the whole place apart?"

"It gives me the creeps," another confessed. "I've always got the feeling that something is watching me when I'm out there in the bush. I spend half of my time looking over my shoulder."

Other men, too, said that they often had the feeling that something was watching them. These were tough men who had spent much of their lives in wilderness areas. They weren't superstitious, but they weren't happy about the fact that an eight-hundred-pound something-or-other was hanging around in their area. Whatever it was, none of them had ever met one, and they didn't know whether or not it would be friendly.

Several wives also lived in the Bluff Creek camp. They were there alone during the day and they kept loaded rifles close at hand at all times. If the Giant Wild Man decided to pay them a visit, they were ready to give him a warm reception. "If he stops by for lunch, we'll give him a bellyful of lead," declared a young wife, her eyes on the rifle by the door.

Mrs. Jesse Bemis was actually more curious about the creature than she was afraid of it. At first her husband had scoffed at the idea of a giant creature roaming around in the wilderness of northern California. "The last giant in this world was a guy called Goliath and he was killed by a kid named David," he told his wife. After seeing the tracks several times, however, he had to admit that there was something very, very strange indeed prowling around at night.

The more Mrs. Bemis thought about the creature, the more curious she became. Something had made those enormous footprints and she was determined to find out what that something was. Nobody in camp was able to tell her anything, so she decided to try elsewhere. Sitting down at her kitchen table, she wrote a brief report of what had been happening around the Bluff Creek camp and sent the report to the leading local newspaper, *The Humboldt Times* in Eureka. "Have you ever heard of anything like this before?" she inquired of the editor.

Andrew Genzoli, editor of *The Humboldt Times*, had been a newspaperman all his life. He had dealt with plenty of quacks, cranks, and pranksters, but Mrs. Bemis's letter intrigued him. She wasn't seeking publicity and she was obviously sincere. Although editor Genzoli knew that he could expect a storm of ridicule if he published the letter, he decided to do so anyway. His own curiosity had been aroused, and he hoped that someone might be able to throw some light on the matter.

To Genzoli's complete astonishment, there was no ridicule whatsoever. On the contrary, people from several northern California counties came forward with information. Many of them had seen enormous footprints in one place or another. Some of these had been an incredible twenty-two inches long.

There were even a number of eyewitness reports from people who asked that their names not be revealed. In every case, the descriptions were alike in almost every detail. The creatures were completely covered with hair, were anywhere from seven to ten feet tall, and weighed somewhere between seven hundred and one thousand pounds. They vaguely resembled giant, hair-covered humans and always walked in an upright position.

Andrew Genzoli studied the reports and wondered what action to take. Did he dare tell the world that such oddities were roaming freely around in the wilds of northern California? he asked himself.

3

Several days after editor Andrew Genzoli had published Mrs. Jesse Bemis's letter, Jerry Crew arrived in Eureka. Bigfoot, as the men were now calling the giant creature, had again been making his rounds. Crew had made plaster-of-paris casts of both the left and right foot and brought them into Eureka to show them to a friend.

Someone told Genzoli about it and he rushed over to see for himself. What he saw nearly bowled him over. He had stepped straight into an almost unbelievable story, and he knew it. The next day's edition of *The Humboldt Times* carried a front-page photo of Bigfoot's footprints and a full report of the strange goings-on at the Bluff Creek camp.

October 14, 1958, marks the day that made Bigfoot world-famous. Genzoli's story was picked up by the news services and printed in virtually every important paper in the United States and abroad. So many letters and cables of inquiry came flooding into the *Times*'s office that poor Genzoli almost wished he had never heard of Bigfoot.

Many of the inquiries came from people who were genuinely interested in the subject and wanted more information. The idea of great hairy giants roaming around in the American forests appealed to them.

Giants are fascinating fellows and it was nice to think that there were still a few of them around.

Naturally enough, a great number of people pooh-poohed Genzoli's article. A Hollywood hoax, said some. A story like that could only come from California, declared others. Maybe King Kong is on the loose again, suggested one wit. If such things do exist in America, a woman wrote, then California is the right place for them.

The letters were usually written in a spirit of fun, and a number of them were highly amusing. The one below is typical of several received in the office of the *Times*.

2391 Yeti Drive
Tondup Glacier
Lhasa, Tibet

October 17, 1958

Editor
The Humboldt Times
Eureka, California
United States of America

Dear Sir,

My wife and I found your article on the front page of the *Humboldt Times* of October 14 very interesting. After reading the story and studying the photographs of the footprints, we have come to the conclusion that Bigfoot is actually our son, Hilbert, who ran away from home several million years ago. Hilbert was always very interested in machinery, which is another reason to believe that Bigfoot is our missing son.

We have thought for a time that Hilbert may

have become extinct, so you may well imagine how happy we are to learn that he is alive and well—even if he is in California.

Please don't be frightened when you meet Hilbert. Although he's a big boy, he's actually very shy and gentle. Give him our love and tell him to hurry home. He's been gone for such a long time and we miss him terribly.

Thank you for your kind attention to this matter.

Yours sincerely,
A. Bominable Snowman.

Scientists who read Genzoli's articles chuckled to themselves and promptly forgot about it. Creatures like Bigfoot did not exist in the wilderness of northern California, they reasoned, because creatures like Bigfoot did not exist anywhere on earth. The Age of Giants was a thing of the past.

Ivan T. Sanderson, however, was an exception. Sanderson was a writer and zoological scientist who was particularly interested in manlike monsters. As soon as he heard about Bigfoot, he rushed out to the West Coast to get firsthand information. What he learned made a very deep impression upon him.

It was impossible for the scientist to doubt the words of Jerry Crew and others at the Bluff Creek camp. Their sincerity left no room for doubt. He also talked to several people who claimed to have seen Bigfoot and was convinced that they had seen something entirely out of the ordinary. The tracks, he concluded, could not have been made by a normal man or a machine. That meant, then, that they had been made by either an animal, an abnormal man, or a creature somewhere between the two.

Sanderson very cautiously suggested that Bigfoot might possibly be a humanoid; that is, a cross between man and what we call an animal. The remains of gigantic humanlike apes eight to twelve feet tall had been unearthed in China. Could some of these have survived? he asked himself. Mammoths, mastodons, and other animals had crossed from the Old World to the New World in the Northern Hemisphere. If they had done it, then why couldn't ape-men or humanoids have done so, too?

Assuming that these creatures had survived, where would they live? The answer to that one was easy. They would live in places not populated by modern man. Places like the unmapped and uninhabited forested slopes of northern California. There was plenty of water, there was enough to eat, and there was no one to bother them.

Rugged, almost inaccessible country like the Bluff Creek area ought to suit a Bigfoot family just fine, Sanderson reasoned.

Although Bigfoot didn't know it, he had made a bitter enemy. Ray Wallace, the man who had contracted to build the Bluff Creek road for the public works department, had been away on a business trip and had heard only vague rumors of what was going on. When he returned to Eureka and found out a few facts, he flew into a rage. "Somebody," he thundered, "is trying to mess up my operation!"

Wallace had good reason to be upset. Skilled and reliable workers were hard to find in Humboldt County. Few men enjoyed working and living in a place as remote as the Bluff Creek area and he'd had trouble hiring a full crew. He had believed, though, that those he had hired would stay on until the job was finished. Now he learned that one man after another was packing up and returning to civilization. Something had gone wrong somewhere and Wallace was determined to solve the mystery.

"What's all this Bigfoot business about, anyway?" Ray demanded of his brother, Wilbur, who had been on the cite since the beginning. "What's going on around this place? Why can't you keep the men on the job?"

Bigfoot had been behaving rather badly the last week or so, and Wilbur Wallace had a very interesting story to tell. His men had reported one morning that a nearly full fifty-five-gallon drum of diesel fuel that had been left standing beside the road had disappeared. Wilbur went to investigate and found that Bigfoot had been there the night before. The tracks went down the road, then turned off into the brush toward a steep ravine. At the bottom of the ravine, Wilbur found the oil drum. It had rolled down the bank after having been thrown from the top.

"But—but—" Ray Wallace blurted, "but a nearly full drum of diesel must weigh three or four hundred pounds! Surely . . ."

"Oh, that's only a part of it." Wilbur couldn't quite

keep the grin off his face. "He came back again the following night, dragged some steel culvert from the dump, and tossed it off a cliff."

"Bigfoot's last trick," Wilbur went on, the grin a bit wider, "was to make off with a tire from an earth-mover. One of those things weighs over two hundred fifty pounds, you know, but he hurled it into a ravine like a man throwing a rock."

The unfortunate Ray Wallace was hopping mad. All the married men had left the job because they felt their wives were in danger. Three bulldozers were sitting idle because there were no men to operate them. The enitre brush-cutting crew had quit and more men were talking about going home. Bigfoot had almost stopped the Bluff Creek road-building project.

"I'll fix that rascal," Ray Wallace vowed to his brother. "I'll fix him for once and always. You just see if I don't."

5

Ray Wallace's proposed solution to the problem was really quite simple. He hired two hunters named Ray Kerr and Bob Breazele and gave them their instructions. "Get Bigfoot," he ordered them. "I don't care who he is or what he is, but he's ruining my business and I want him shot."

Bob Breazele had hunted professionally in Mexico

and other places. He owned an enormous British-made gun that really impressed the locals. He also owned four good dogs. "These dogs ain't afraid of nothing," he told Wallace. "If they see a rhinoceros out there in the brush, they'll go straight for him."

As luck would have it, Bigfoot was sighted just the day before Kerr and Breazele arrived at Bluff Creek. The man's face was as white as the snow on the mountain peaks when he came charging back to camp. "I saw Bigfoot!" he gasped. "He's enormous! Ten feet tall, maybe, and all covered wtih hair. Scared me half to death, he did! Bigger than a gorilla, and arms that hang all the way down to his knees. He was drinking from the creek when I came up, and he rushed off into the brush as soon as he saw me." After telling his story, the man packed his suitcase and collected his pay. "I'm not staying around this place any longer," he told Wilbur Wallace. "I've had enough."

Kerr and Breazele soon learned that hunting Bigfoot was a much tougher job than they had imagined. It wasn't too difficult to find tracks. Following them, though, was another story. Most of the countryside seemed to be either straight up or straight down. Head-high tangles of underbrush didn't make things any easier. It was so thick in many places that even the four dogs had trouble fighting their way through. Bigfoot, of course, didn't have the slightest difficulty. He sliced his way through the forest as a hot knife slices through butter.

And then one night they saw it! They were driving slowly back to camp after dark when they suddenly saw this gigantic human-shaped creature, all covered with brown hair, squatting by the road. Bigfoot wasn't in the mood for company that night, however.

Leaping to his feet, he crossed the road in two strides and disappeared into the forest.

The two hunters weren't about to go after their quarry in the dark, and no one can blame them for that. They did, however, do some measuring and discovered that Bigfoot had covered exactly twenty feet in two strides. And he had started from a squatting position!

Understandably, both Kerr and Breazele were wildly excited. "It all happened so fast that it's hard to give a really close description," Ray Kerr told the men at the camp. "It ran upright like a man, but I don't think it was human. I've never seen anything like it before in my life. It was all covered with hair, it had long, swinging arms, and it looked to me like it was eight or ten feet tall."

Breazele's description was exactly the same, but he added, "It wasn't a man. I don't know what it was, but it wasn't a man and that's definite."

First light found the hunters and the dogs at the spot where they had seen Bigfoot the night before. The dogs picked up the scent and took off at once. Kerr and Breazele struggled down the slope after them. It wasn't long before the men realized that all was not as it should be. The dogs had simply disappeared without a trace. There was no answering barks when Breazele called and whistled. The two men spent several more hours searching, then returned to camp in confusion.

The next day an Indian named Curtis Mitchell arrived at the Bluff Creek camp with a strange story. He was working on a bridge a few miles away, and for some reason he had wandered off into the forest. There he found the bodies of four dogs that had literally been torn to pieces.

"Did you see any tracks?" someone asked.

"I didn't stick around to look," the Indian replied. "I got out of there as fast as I could."

6

Although the unlucky Ray Wallace finally managed to get his road built, Bigfoot was by no means forgotten. Letters of inquiry and reports of sightings still came pouring into Andrew Genzoli's office. Most people told about giant footprints they had discovered, but a few had seen Bigfoot himself. Several of the stories lead one to believe that Bigfoot either has a sense of humor or is a bit of a rascal. "He's also a thief," says Gary Joanis.

Gary should know. He and Jim Newall shot a deer in a clearing. They were just walking over to get it, when "a giant, human-like form came out of some brush not more than a hundred feet away." Gary and Jim stood rooted to the spot. The creature picked up the deer, tucked it under his arm, and walked back into the brush with tremendously long strides. "It wasn't an inch less than nine feet tall and it was all covered with dark hair," says Joanis. "It made a very strange whistling scream that we could still hear long after the thing had disappeared."

Benjamin Wilder, too, reported a harrowing experi-

ence. He was dead tired after putting in a lot of over-
time and decided to pull off to the side of the road for
a little nap. He had no sooner fallen asleep when his
car was shaken violently. Just an earthquake, Wilder
said to himself, rolling over for forty more winks.
Once again his car received a violent shaking. That's
strange, thought Wilder. If this is an earthquake, I
ought to be able to hear rocks rolling down the moun-
tainside.

Wilder sat up, turned on his flashlight, and gasped
in astonishment. A huge, hairy creature he assumed
was a bear was standing beside the driver's door of the
car. "Beat it!" yelled Wilder. "Get out of here!"

Then the thing did something most unbearlike. It
let forth a piercing, whistling sort of scream and gave
the car another shake. Wilder was terrified. He knew
now that he wasn't dealing with a bear, and he yelled
at the top of his voice and blasted on the horn. This
must have frightened the animal and it ran off down
an incline on its hind legs. "I never saw its face," said
Wilder, "and I'm glad I didn't. The part of it I did
see was bad enough."

Nearly every sighting—whether of prints or of the
creature itself—was reported in newspapers throughout
the country. Men armed with rifles or cameras or both
arrived in the Bluff Creek area for a look around. Dr.
R. Maurice Tripp, a geologist and geophysicist, found
a seventeen-inch footprint and made a cast of it.
"From my engineering studies of the soil properties
and the depth of the footprint," he declared, "I can
safely say that no creature weighing less than eight
hundred pounds could have left a track like that."

Another expert who arrived on the scene was John
Green from British Columbia, Canada. Green is Cana-

da's foremost authority on the sasquatch—which is what Canadians call an Abominable Snowman or Bigfoot. He has been studying the sasquatch for years and has written three books about it. His reason for coming to California was to compare tracks and collect information. "There can be no doubt at all about it," he concluded after a detailed study. "Bigfoot and sasquatch are one and the same fellow."

The search for Bigfoot really got off to a big start with the organization of the Pacific Northwest Expedition. This group of men had one great advantage over all the others. It was sponsored by two Texas millionaires, Tom Slick and Kirk Johnson, and had all the money it needed.

Slick and Johnson had also sponsored three expeditions to Nepal in search of Abominable Snowmen. It was Tom Slick's belief that the creature reported in the Humboldt County wilderness was closely related to the creature he had searched for in the Himalayas. "It's our intention to photograph and definitely prove the existence and identification of the creature," stated Slick. "If we can do that, it could be one of the most important scientific events of all times."

Ivan T. Sanderson, the writer and zoological scientist who had rushed out to California when he first heard about Bigfoot, was a member of Slick's Pacific Northwest Expedition. "I'd like to make one thing clear before we start out," he announced to the group. "We are not going after an Abominable Snowman. That's an absolutely incorrect term and I hate to hear it used." The scientist paused a moment, then went on: "In the first place, we have no right to call these creatures 'abominable.' In the second place, they don't live in the snow. In the third place, we don't even know for sure that these creatures are actually men."

That said, the Pacific Northwest Expedition took off into the unexplored and uninhabited wilderness of northern California.

7

Many strange letters crossed Andrew Genzoli's desk that fall, but one in particular really made him sit up and take notice. He published it to amuse his readers, then began to have second thoughts about the matter. Truth can often be stranger than fiction, and it would be hard to imagine anything stranger than the letter reproduced below:

Editor's Mail Box
RR5 Langley, British Columbia

Editor
The Humboldt Times
Eureka, California

Dear Sir,

I am interested in an article in the *Agassiz Advance* about tracks seen in California. Have you any pictures of these footprints or some description of them that you could send me? I claim to be the only living man that's seen a Sasquatch. In fact I was kidnapped by one and lived with them for about six days before I got away from them. I claim they are human beings that for one reason or other got left behind from our civilization, but it's one thing about their feet that is not like a human foot today. I saw their feet close up. In the family that kidnapped me was one old man, one old lady, one boy, and one girl. So I guess I know what kind of feet they have, old or young. Your guess about size is about right. It's hard to estimate when you have nothing to compare them with. I always estimated that the old man like I call him would be about 8 feet tall and weight about 800 pounds, a hundred more or less.

I hope to hear from you.

Sincerely,
Albert Ostman.

Genzoli decided that the letter was simply too far-fetched to have been written by a crank. It was so unusual that there had to be a ring of truth in it somewhere. Ostman had read about the tracks in the Canadian newspaper_ Agassiz_ Advance, and John Green, Canada's foremost authority on the sasquatch, was the editor of the Advance. Moreover, Agassiz was across the Fraser River from Langley, where Ostman was now living. With a little sigh of relief, Genzoli put Ostman's letter into an envelope and mailed it to British Columbia.

The letter came as no surprise to John Green. He had talked to a radio announcer the year before who had interviewed Ostman and was convinced that his story was actually true. Green also went to see Ostman. The old man's story defied all belief. Such things just didn't happen. And yet the sasquatch expert confessed that he had to accept Ostman's unbelievable story as the truth. Unless a man had actually lived with the sasquatches, Green reasoned, he couldn't possibly know so much about them.

Surely Albert Ostman's account of being kidnapped by a sasquatch must rank as one of the most unusual stories of the century.

In the summer of 1924, Albert Ostman was prospecting in the mountains of British Columbia. One morning he noticed that something had gone through his camp while he had been sleeping, but nothing seemed to be missing. The same thing happened the following night. This time, however, his packsack, which had been hanging on a branch, had been turned upside down and his visitor had taken some preserves and pancake flour.

The third night, Ostman promised himself that he'd be ready for his intruder. After securely buckling the straps on his packsack, he crawled into his sleeping bag. He was fully clothed and his rifle was beside him. He intended to stay awake all night and find out exactly who his visitor was. In spite of his good intentions, he fell asleep almost at once.

Sometime during the middle of the night, Ostman had a rude awakening. He felt himself being picked up while still in his sleeping bag. Then he had the sensation of being slung over someone's shoulder.

What's going on here? he asked himself, trying desperately to keep his wits about him. What's happening?

Whatever it was that had picked Ostman up now began walking at a very rapid pace. It breathed heavily and gave a slight cough when going up steep slopes. Going downhill, the creature dragged the sleeping bag behind him and moved even more rapidly. On the relatively level stretches, it seemed to be going at a trot.

Poor Ostman was desperately unhappy. He was also horribly uncomfortable. "I was all hunched down on the bottom of the sleeping bag and I couldn't move," he recalls. "I was sitting on my feet and my legs ached terribly. My sheath knife was underneath me and I couldn't get at it or I could have cut my way out."

Almost all of Ostman's life had been spent logging and prospecting in the mountains and forests of British Columbia. Although he had heard countless stories about the sasquatch, he steadfastly refused to believe any of them. Even though he had seen their tracks and heard their high-pitched wailing whistles, he could not convince himself that such creatures actually existed. "When I was in that sleeping bag, though," he now says, "I knew that it was a sasquatch that was carrying me because there was no other creature that could do it."

After what Ostman guessed to be about three hours of fast traveling, they finally reached their destination. The sasquatch dropped the packsack first, then the sleeping bag. Ostman pulled himself out, but his legs were so numb that he couldn't stand up. Although it was still dark, he could see four creatures standing around him. They chattered constantly while Ostman massaged his legs.

The numbness in his legs finally subsided and the prospector struggled to his feet, his hands firmly gripping his rifle. "What do you fellows want with me?" he asked in a quaking voice "What're you going to do with me?"

The only answer was another babble of chattering.

9

Daylight comes early in the northern latitudes in summer, and it was quite light by five o'clock. Ostman was now able to get a good look at his captors. They were all covered with hair and wore no clothes at all. He believed that they were a family group—father, mother, son, and daughter. The boy and girl seemed to be afraid of him. The mother didn't appear to be at all pleased with what her husband had dragged home. The old man, however, was apparently very proud of his conquest. He waved his arms about at a great rate and chattered nonstop.

Escape was the first thing that came to Ostman's mind. As the sun got higher, he saw that he was in a small valley surrounded by high mountains. On the southeast side there was a V-shaped opening, and he guessed that was the only way to get in or out of the valley. The old man seemed to know what his prisoner was thinking. Leaving the group, he marched over to the opening and sat down. Well, that takes care of that, Ostman sighed.

Except for the fact that the old man guarded the

opening, Ostman was free to wander about as he pleased. He moved his belongings under two cypress trees beside the canyon wall and took stock of his situation. It wasn't good. He didn't know where he was. He had only six shells left for his rifle, which had been in his sleeping bag. The packsack contained only enough food for a week, and most important, he didn't know what the sasquatch intended to do with him. This was what worried him most.

The next morning the prospector decided to leave the place even if he had to shoot his way out. Shouldering his packsack, he picked up his rifle and headed for the opening in the wall. The old man immediately leaped to his feet and held up his hands as though to push him back.

"Get out of the way," Ostman ordered, his rifle aimed at the giant's head. "I'm going through."

The old man grunted something and again pushed his hand toward him.

"I'm going through," Ostman insisted, his rifle at the ready.

There was another grunt and the giant took a menacing step toward Ostman, both hands extended.

The prospector hesitated. His .30–30 rifle was fine for deer, but did it have enough power to stop the sasquatch? It wasn't hard to imagine what would happen if the bullets only wounded him. Besides, the idea of murdering the manlike creature wasn't to his liking. There must be another way of getting out of here, Ostman decided, and walked unhappily back to his camp under the cypress trees.

10

While planning his escape, Ostman made a close study of the sasquatch family. This is a description of them in his own words:

> The old lady was a meek old thing. The young fellow was by this time quite friendly. The girl would not hurt anybody. Her chest was flat like a boy's—no development like young ladies.
>
> The young fellow might have been between 11–18 years old, about seven feet tall and might weigh about 300 pounds. His chest would be 50–55 inches, his waist about 36–38 inches. He had wide jaws and a narrow forehead that slanted upward round at the back about four or five inches higher than the forehead. The hair on their heads was about six inches long. The hair on the rest of the body was short and thick in places. The women's hair was a bit longer on their heads and the hair on the forehead had an upward turn like bangs. The old lady was over seven feet tall and would be about 500–600 pounds.
>
> She had very wide hips and a gooselike walk. She was not built for beauty or speed. A brassiere would have been a great improvement on her looks and her figure.

The man's eyeteeth were longer than the rest of the teeth, but not long enough to be called tusks. The old man must have been eight feet tall. Big barrel chest and big hump on his back and powerful shoulders. His biceps on his upper arm were enormous and tapered down to his elbows. His forearms were longer than common people have, but well proportioned. His hands were wide, the palm was long and broad and hollow like a scoop. His fingers were short in proportion to the rest of his hand. His fingernails were like chisels. The only place they had no hair was inside their hands and the soles of their feet and upper part of the nose and eyelids. I never did see their ears because hair was hanging over them.

If the old man were to wear a collar, it would have to be at least 30 inches. I have no idea what size shoes they would need. I was watching the young fellow's foot one day when he was sitting down. The soles of his feet seemed to be padded like a dog's foot and the big toe was longer than the rest and very strong. In mountain climbing, all he needed was footing for his big toe. They were very agile. To sit, they turned their knees out and came straight down. To rise, they came straight up without help of their arms or hands.

The old lady and the boy did most of the food-gathering. The family lived on a type of grass with long sweet roots, nuts, berries, twigs of various kinds, and plants that Ostman was unable to identify. Whether or not they ever ate meat the prospector didn't know. He thought that the old man might be the hunter but couldn't go out after game because he had to guard his captive.

Naturally enough, Ostman wondered whether the family might not be saving him for one of their Sunday dinners. There didn't seem to be any other reason for capturing him and holding him prisoner. This thought did very little to cheer him up.

Like many woodsmen, Ostman took snuff regularly. One afternoon he gave a nearly empty can of it to the boy to see what would happen. The young fellow tasted it, made a wry face, and then carried it to his father. The old man seemed to like it. After finishing the tiny bit in the can, he licked the bottom with his tongue. From then on, Ostman gave the old man a pinch or two of snuff each day. A plan was forming in his mind and he knew that he was doomed if it didn't work.

On the morning of the sixth day, the prospector had his first pot of coffee since his capture. Using the labels from his cans, some moss he had dried in the sun, and a few dry twigs he had gathered, he managed to make a fire large enough to get his pot boiling. The aroma of the boiling coffee interested the old man and the boy and they squatted down about ten feet away from their prisoner.

Ostman's heart was in his throat as he ate his few remaining biscuits and drank his coffee. He was about to put his plan into effect and it had to work. When he finished his breakfast, he opened a new can of snuff. He took a tiny pinch between his thumb and index finger, then offered the can to the old man.

He did exactly as the prospector had expected. Seizing the can, he emptied the entire thing into his mouth and swallowed it in one gulp. "It was a terribly cruel trick to play on him," Ostman admits, "but I didn't want to shoot him and have murder on my conscience."

Within seconds, the old man was deathly sick. His eyes rolled in his head and he began to squeal in agony. Grabbing the pot of scalding coffee, he drank it down grounds and all. It didn't help. The pulverized tobacco had turned his stomach into a flaming furnace. After writhing and rolling about on the floor of the valley for several minutes, the old man got to his feet and started staggering toward the spring for some water.

This is it! Ostman exclaimed to himself. It's now or never! It took him only a few seconds to gather his belongings together and head for the opening at the bottom of the valley. He just made it. The old woman let out a piercing scream and rushed after him. As he came through the opening, Ostman fired a shot over her head. She screamed again, turned around, and dashed back into the valley.

Albert Ostman was safe, but thirty-three years passed before he ever told anyone the almost unbelievable story of being kidnapped by a sasquatch. "Who would have believed me?" he asks.

11

In the same year that Albert Ostman's story was released to the public by John Green, British Columbia was getting ready to celebrate its one-hundredth birthday. The village council of Harrison Hot Springs met and decided that it would do something to publicize some aspect of life in the province. A sasquatch hunt was suggested, and the idea was greeted with great enthusiasm. After all, sasquatch tracks had frequently been seen in the surrounding forests and there had been a number of sightings.

John Green, Canada's sasquatch authority, served a term as mayor of Harrison Hot Springs. He rather liked the idea and gave it a lot of publicity in his newspaper, the *Agassiz-Harrison Advance*. Others, too, looked upon it as a unique venture, and papers all over Canada and the United States carried the story.

Not everyone, though was in favor of the project and, after much debate, the Harrison Hot Springs sasquatch hunt never took place. It did, however, arouse a great deal of interest in the hairy giants that roam about in the mountains of British Columbia. It also brought to John Green a visitor who had a most unusual story to tell:

William Roe had been brought up in the north woods of Michigan. He was fascinated by wild animals and spent all his spare time studying their lives and habits. After finishing school, he went to Canada and supported himself by hunting and trapping. Later he took a job with a road-building gang in British Columbia.

One Sunday in October, 1955, Roe decided to climb up Mica Mountain. It meant a five-mile walk, but he had nothing else to do. There was a deserted mine near the top of the mountain and he thought he'd take a look at that.

He came in sight of the mine about three o'clock. He had been walking through low brush, but there was a clearing in front of him. In the brush on the far side of the clearing he saw what he first thought was a grizzly bear. Although it was only about seventy-five yards away, Roe had no desire to shoot it. Instead, he sat down on a rock and watched, his rifle resting across his knees.

From his sitting position, he could just see part of the animal's head and the top of one shoulder. A moment later, it stepped out into the opening and Roe almost rolled off his rock. The creature wasn't a bear. It wasn't, in fact, like anything Roe had ever seen before.

While Roe stared in utter amazement, the creature came across the clearing and headed straight toward him. It walked like a man, but as it came closer Roe could tell by the breasts that it was a female. It was about seven feet tall, three feet across the shoulders, and weighed about five hundred pounds. Dark-brown hair covered it from head to foot. Its arms were much thicker than a man's and reached almost to its knees. When it walked, it placed the heel down first and Roe could see the gray-brown skin on the soles of the feet.

The creature came to the edge of the bush Roe was now hiding in and squatted down within twenty feet of him. Reaching out its hands, it pulled the branches of bushes toward it and stripped off the leaves with strong white teeth. It was obviously having its lunch.

Roe was much too fascinated to be frightened. He was certain that he was seeing an animal virtually unknown to science and he studied it closely. The creature's head, he told John Green, was higher at the back than at the front. The nose was broad and flat; the lips and chin protruded farther than its nose. The hair covering it was only about an inch long and the hair on the face was even shorter. Its ears were shaped like a human's ears, but its neck was entirely unhuman. It was shorter and much thicker than the neck of any man Roe had ever seen.

Several long minutes passed before the creature finally spotted Roe. It parted some bushes and found itself staring straight into the man's eyes. A look of complete astonishment appeared on its face. Still in a crouched position, it backed up three or four short steps, then straightened up to its full height and began walking rapidly away. It kept watching the man over its shoulder, but it seemed to be more curious than afraid.

A sudden thought flashed through Roe's mind. If I shoot this animal, he reflected, I'll probably have a specimen of great interest to the scientific world. Raising his rifle, he took careful aim at the back of the creature's head. Just at that moment, the thing turned around again and took another look. Roe sighed and lowered his rifle. "I just couldn't do it," he reported. "It looked so much like a human being that I knew I would never forgive myself if I killed it."

When the creature reached the far side of the clearing, it threw its head back and made a peculiar noise that Roe could only describe as a whinny. Then it walked through the brush and into the forest. Roe saw it again when it came out on a small ridge a couple of hundred yards away. Once again it threw back its head and made the same weird whinnying sound before disappearing around a corner.

"Whether this creature was a sasquatch or an Abominable Snowman or a Bigfoot or what, I just don't know," Roe admits. "I had never seen anything like it before and what it was that I saw will always remain a mystery to me."

"I hate to sound bloodthirsty," John Green said when I was visiting him at his home in Harrison Hot

Springs, "but I think William Roe should have shot this creature. We've got to give the scientific world some concrete evidence that these animals or subhumans actually exist. If we can't capture one alive, then I think one should be shot."

12

While digging up background material on the hairy giants, John Green discovered that one of them actually *had* been captured. The case was fully documented and nobody could doubt that it was true. The creature had been captured in British Columbia less than one hundred miles from the United States border. The story appeared in the *Daily Colonist* and this is what it said:

WHAT IS IT?
A STRANGE CREATURE CAPTURED ABOVE YALE
A BRITISH COLUMBIA GORILLA

Yale, B.C., July 3rd, 1882.

In the immediate vicinity of No. 4 tunnel, situated some 20 miles above the village, are bluffs of rocks which have hitherto been unsurmountable, but on Monday morning last were successfully scaled by Mr. Onderdonk's employees on the regular train from Lytton. Assisted by Mr. Costerton, The British Columbia's Express Company's messenger, a number of gentlemen from Lytton and points east of that place, after considerable trouble and perilous climbing captured a creature who may truly be called half man and half beast. "Jacko," as the creature has been called by his captors, is something of the gorilla type standing about 4 feet 7 inches in height and weighing 127 pounds. He has long black strong hair and resembles a human being with one exception, his entire body, excepting his hands (or paws) and feet are covered with glossy hair about one inch long. His forearm is much longer than a man's forearm, and he possesses enormous strength, as he will take hold of a stick and break it by wrenching or twisting it, which no living man could do in the same way. Since his capture he is very reticent, only occasionally uttering a noise which is half bark and half growl. He is, however, becoming daily more attached to his keeper, Mr. George Telbury, of this place, who proposes shortly starting for London, England, to exhibit him. His favorite food so far is berries, and he drinks fresh milk with evident relish. By advice of Dr. Hannington, raw meats have been withheld from Jacko, as the doctor thinks it would have a tendency to make him savage.

The mode of capture was as follows: Ned Austin, the engineer, on coming in sight of the bluff at eastern end of No. 4 tunnel saw what he supposed to be a man lying asleep at close proximity to the track, and, as quick as thought, blew the signal to apply the brakes. The brakes were instantly applied, and in a few seconds the train was brought to a standstill. At this moment, the supposed man sprang up, and uttering a sharp quick bark, began to climb the steep bluff. Conductor R. J. Craig and express messenger Costerton, followed by the baggage man and the brakesmen, jumped from the train and knowing they were some 20 minutes ahead of time, immediately gave chase.

After 5 minutes of perilous climbing the then supposed demented Indian was corralled on a projecting shelf of rock where he could neither ascend nor descend. The query now was how to capture him alive, which was quickly decided by Mr. Craig, who crawled on his hands and knees until he was about 40 feet above the creature. Taking a small piece of loose rock he let it fall and it had the desired effect of rendering poor Jacko incapable of resistance for a time at least. The bell rope was then brought up and Jacko was now lowered to terra firma. After firmly binding him and placing him in the baggage car, "off brakes" was sounded and the train started for Yale. At the station a large crowd who had heard of the capture by telephone from Spuzzum Flat were assembled, and each one anxious to have the first look at the monstrosity, but they were disappointed, as Jacko had been taken off at the machine shop and placed in charge of his present keeper.

The question naturally arises, how came the creature where it was first seen by Mr. Austin? From bruises about its head and body, and apparent soreness since its capture, it is supposed that Jacko returned too near the edge of the bluff, slipped, fell and lay where found until the sound of the rushing train aroused him. Mr. Thomas White, and Mr. Gorian, as well as Mr. Major, who kept a small store about half a mile west of the tunnel during the past two years, have mentioned having seen a curious creature at different points between Camps 13 and 17, but no attention was paid to their remarks as people came to the conclusion that they had seen either a bear or stray Indian dog. Who can unravel the mystery that now surrounds Jacko? Does he belong to a species hitherto unknown in this part of the continent?

The reporter who wrote this article did a good job. Later investigations proved that all the people mentioned in the story were genuine. The railroad played an important part in the opening up and development of lower British Columbia, and the men mentioned were all well known. The reporter, moreover, appears to be perfectly accurate when he states that, except for the fact that the creature was all covered with hair, it resembled a human being.

So what sort of a creature was Jacko? Well, he definitely wasn't a naughty boy who had run away from home. Neither was he an ape of some sort that had escaped from a zoo or circus. Nor was he an Indian that had gone berserk, as the train crew first supposed. In the light of what we now know, it's probably safe to say that Jacko was a little sasquatch who got himself into a whole mess of trouble.

The sad part of this story is that nobody knows what happened to poor little Jacko. The article tells us that Mr. George Telbury planned to take the little fellow to England and put him on exhibit. Well, Jacko never got to England. We can be sure of that. If he had arrived there safely, one great scientific problem would have been solved.

It appears, then, that one of two things must have happened to our friend Jacko. Either he died or he escaped from Mr. Telbury and disappeared into the wilderness.

13

People sometimes ask why it is that the early trappers, prospectors, and mountain men who explored the American West never reported seeing or hearing about an Abominable Snowman or a Bigfoot. Well, the answer to that question is that they did. Interestingly enough, one of the earliest sightings is reported in Theodore Roosevelt's book *Wilderness Hunter*, which he wrote in 1892. Teddy, as every schoolboy knows—or should know—was a rugged young outdoorsman who later became the twenty-sixth President of the United States.

Here is the story as related by Roosevelt in *Wilderness Hunter*:

It was told to me by a grizzled, weatherbeaten old mountain hunter, named Bauman, who was born and had passed all his life on the frontier. He must have believed what he said, for he could hardly repress a shudder at certain points of the tale.

When the event occurred Bauman was still a young man, and was trapping with a partner among the mountains dividing the forks of the Salmon from the head of Wisdom River. Not having had much luck, he and his partner determined to go up into a particularly wild and lonely pass through which ran a small stream said to contain many beaver. The pass had an evil reputation because the year before a solitary hunter who had wandered into it was there slain, seemingly by a wild beast, the half-eaten remains being afterwards found by some mining prospectors who had passed his camp only the night before.

The memory of this event, however, weighed very lightly with the two trappers, who were as adventurous and hardy as others of their kind. They then struck out on foot through the vast, gloomy forest, and in about four hours reached a little open glade where they concluded to camp, as signs of game were plentiful.

There was still an hour or two of daylight left, and after building a brush lean-to and throwing down and opening their packs they started upstream.

At dusk they again reached camp.

They were surprised to find that during their absence something, apparently a bear, had visited camp, and had rummaged about among their things, scattering the contents of their packs, and in sheer wantonness destroying their lean-to. The footprints of the beast were quite plain, but at first they paid no particular heed to them, busying themselves with rebuilding the lean-to, laying out their beds and stores, and lighting the fire.

While Bauman was making ready supper, it being already dark, his companion began to examine the tracks more closely, and soon took a brand from the fire to follow them up, where the intruder had walked along a game trail after leaving the camp. Coming back to the fire, he stood by it a minute or two, peering out into the darkness, and suddenly remarked, "Bauman, that bear has been walking on two legs."

Bauman laughed at this, but his partner insisted that he was right, and upon examining the tracks with a torch, they certainly did seem to be made by but two paws or feet. However, it was too dark to make sure. After discussing whether the footprints could possibly be those of a human being, and coming to the conclusion that they could not be, the two men rolled up in their blankets, and went to sleep under the lean-to.

At midnight, Bauman was awakened by some noise, and sat up in his blankets. As he did so his nostrils were struck by a strong, wild-beast odor, and he caught the loom of a great body in the darkness at the mouth of the lean-to. Grasping his rifle, he fired at the vague, threatening shadow, but must have missed, for immediately afterwards he heard the smashing of the underbrush as the thing, whatever it was, rushed off into the impenetrable blackness of the forest and the night.

After this the two men slept but little, sitting up by the rekindled fire, but they heard nothing more. In the morning they started out to look at the few traps they had set the previous evening and put out new ones. By an unspoken agreement they kept together all day, and returned to camp toward evening.

On nearing it they saw, hardly to their astonishment, that the lean-to had again been torn down. The visitor of the preceding day had returned, and in wanton malice had tossed about their camp kit and bedding, and destroyed the shanty. The ground was marked up by its tracks, and on leaving the camp it had gone along the soft earth by the brook, where the footprints were as clear as on snow, and, after a careful scrutiny of the trail, it certainly did seem as if, whatever the thing was, it had walked off on but two legs.

The men, thoroughly uneasy, gathered a great heap of dead logs, and kept a roaring fire throughout the night, one or the other sitting on guard most of the time. About midnight the thing came down through the forest opposite, across the brook, and stayed there on the hillside for nearly an hour. They could hear the branches crackle as it moved about, and several times it uttered a harsh, grating, long-drawn moan, a peculiarly sinister sound. Yet it did not venture near the fire.

In the morning the two trappers, after discussing the strange events of the last 36 hours, decided that they would shoulder their packs and leave the valley that afternoon.

The whole morning they kept together, picking up trap after trap, each one empty. On first leaving camp they had the disagreeable sensation of being followed. In the dense spruce thickets they occasionally heard a branch snap after they had passed; and now and then there were slight rustling noises among the small pines to one side of them.

At noon they were back within a couple of miles of camp. In the high, bright sunlight their fears seemed absurd to the two armed men, accustomed as they were, through long years of lonely wandering in the wilderness to face every kind of danger from man, brute or element. There were still three beaver traps to collect from a little pond in a wide ravine nearby. Bauman volunteered to gather these and bring them in, while his companion went ahead to camp and made ready the packs.

On reaching the pond Bauman found three beavers in the traps, one of which had been pulled loose and carried into a beaver house. He took several hours in securing and preparing the beaver, and when he started homewards he marked, with some uneasiness, how low the sun was getting.

At last he came to the edge of the glade where the camp lay, and shouted as he approached it, but got no answer. The camp fire had gone out, though the thin blue smoke was still curling upwards.

Near it lay the packs wrapped and arranged. At first Bauman could see nobody; nor did he receive an answer to his call. Stepping forward he again shouted, and as he did so his eyes fell on the body of his friend, stretched beside the trunk of a great fallen spruce. Rushing towards it the horrified trapper found that the body was still warm, but that the neck was broken, while there were four great fang marks in the throat.

The footprints of the unknown beast creature, printed deep in the soft soil, told the whole story.

The unfortunate man, having finished his

packing, had sat down on the spruce log with his
face to the fire, and his back to the dense woods,
to wait for his companion. It was then that the
creature had attacked. It had not eaten the body,
but apparently had romped and gambolled
around it in uncouth, ferocious glee, occasionally
rolling over and over it; and had then fled back
into the soundless depths of the woods.

Bauman, utterly unnerved, and believing that
the creature with which he had to deal was something either half human or half devil, some great
goblin beast, abandoned everything but his rifle
and struck off at great speed down the pass, not
halting until he reached the beaver meadows
where the hobbled ponies were still grazing.
Mounting, he rode onwards through the night,
until far beyond the reach of pursuit.

14

Roosevelt's story as told by the old mountain man is
interesting and no doubt true. It makes us wonder,
though, just what sort of a fellow Bigfoot really is.
Most likely there are both nice ones and naughty ones.

Apparently Bigfoot's ire is easily triggered by any ag-
gressive action toward him on the part of men. This is
probably what happened on the slopes of Mount Saint
Helens in Skamania County, Washington, in the same

year that Albert Ostman was kidnapped by a sasquatch.

Five men were working a mine on the east side of the mountain in particularly rugged terrain. Because they expected to bé there for a long time, they built a very comfortable cabin. It was halfway up the canyon wall on a large ledge of flat rock. To make certain that their cabin could not be damaged by bears, porcupines, or the heavy winter snows, they built the entire thing of solid, ten-inch logs. They couldn't have known it at the time, but the sturdy cabin saved their lives.

Every once in a while, the miners saw huge, naked footprints in the area. Although this didn't really worry them, they seldom went anywhere without their rifles. It seems that they were a rather unimaginative group of men. They knew that nobody lived anywhere near them, yet they had little or no interest in the outsized tracks.

The five men were on their way back to their cabin one evening after work when they saw what they described as "a great hairy ape" peering at them from behind a tree. One of the men threw his rifle to his shoulder and fired a quick shot at the creature's head. He was sure that he had killed it. When they reached the spot, however, there was nothing to be found. Either the man had missed completely or the bullet had merely grazed the head of the animal.

Heavy rain fell all through the hours of darkness and it was still drizzling when the men set off for the mine next morning. Fred Beck was in the lead, his rifle cradled in the crook of his arm. He was approaching the canyon when he suddenly stopped dead in his tracks. A great hairy ape was standing at the very edge of the canyon wall. Beck swiftly fired three shots into the creature's back and the giant tumbled over the cliff into the canyon.

Although the men searched all day, they were unable to find a thing. Torrents of water were coming down off the mountain. The entire floor of the canyon was flooded and the men supposed that the creature had either been washed away or had fallen in some place where it couldn't be reached. The canyon into which the great hairy ape fell appears on the maps today as Ape Canyon, and Fred Beck still has the gun with which he shot the creature.

That night Bigfoot declared war on the five miners. The deep silence of the mountain was shattered by high-pitched whistling screams. Huge boulders began raining down on the roof of the cabin. "It's the apes!" one of the men yelled. "We're being attacked!"

And the attack was a frenzied and furious one. One boulder after another smashed down onto the cabin's roof. Piercing screams echoed through the canyon walls. The men braced the heavy door from inside and fired their rifles, but the barrage of boulders kept falling.

Then the creatures changed their tactics. They jumped up and down on the roof and tried to tear the cabin apart. They hurled themselves against the walls, and one kept smashing against the door. The men were terrified. They weren't at all certain that their cabin would be able to withstand the attack. Neither did they know how many giant hairy apes were attacking them. Fred Beck reported later that there were at the very least two and probably more. The other men thought that there must have been four or five of them. The cabin had no windows and nobody would have been foolish enough to open the door to see how many apes there were.

The attack went on for hour after hour. The terrified men fired their rifles and beat on pots and pans, but it did no good. The angry creatures were determined to destroy the cabin and get at the men inside.

Daylight came at last. The attack ended and the mountain was once again silent. The five men gathered their possessions together and left Mount Saint Helens, the mine, and their cabin behind them as quickly as possible.

Not a single one of them ever went back.

15

People reacted differently to the story told by the five miners. "Man, you fellows must really have been drunk," one said to Fred Beck. The remark made Beck so furious that he threatened to blow the man's head off.

It was obvious to everyone, of course, that the miners had had a terrifying experience of some kind. They were tough men who didn't scare easily. They were at home in the gloomy forests and lonely mountain ranges. Bears and wolves didn't worry them, but whatever it was that had attacked them had frightened them out of their wits. Although they had been working a profitable mine, none of them wanted anything more to do with it. They didn't even go back to their cabin to collect the rest of their possessions. "Whoever wants that mine and that cabin can have them," one announced. "I wouldn't go back up there again for all the tea in China."

The miners' story attracted a great deal of attention. If one man had told it, he would probably have been regarded as someone who was a little soft in the head. In this case, though, the story was told by five hard-headed outdoorsmen, and they all told exactly the same tale.

Like it or not, people had to admit that there were some awfully unusual creatures running around on Mount Saint Helens. It was ridiculous to suppose that the five men had made up the wild story for reasons of their own. It was even more ridiculous to think that they had all dreamed the same dream. Besides, men in lonely cabins high in the mountains never dream about giant hairy apes. They dream about pretty girls and things like that.

The newspapers gave the story of the attack a big play, and reporters, law-enforcement officers, and a few who were just curious formed a posse and went up Mount Saint Helens to have a look around. They came away convinced that the five miners had had a bad night. The cabin had taken a severe beating and numerous large boulders lay all around it. Although they didn't see any giant hairy apes, they saw plenty of huge footprints.

As so often happens, the story told by the five miners brought forth other stories. Indians said that there had been "mountain devils" in the area long before the white men had come to the Pacific Northwest. Old-timers nodded their heads sagely. They had heard about these things years ago and several had seen them. Reporters went through their newspaper files and found that Abominable Snowmen or something similar had been sighted by quite a number of people.

The descriptions were pretty much the same and the observers could just as well have been describing sasquatch or Bigfoot. Today, in fact, the creatures are never called mountain devils or giant hairy apes. It's apparent that the creatures seen in Skamania County, Washington, are identical to those seen in northern California, Oregon, and British Columbia, so the name Bigfoot is used throughout our Pacific Northwest, while the Canadians insist upon calling them sasquatch.

16

Beautiful Mount Saint Helens was the scene of another mystery that attracted worldwide attention in 1950.

A young man named Jim Carter was a member of a skiing and mountaineering group from Seattle. This group had climbed the mountain on a warm, clear Sunday in May. Carter was an amateur photographer as well as an expert skier, and he left the other climbers near a landmark called Dog's Head at about the 8,000-foot level. "I'll go around to the left and get some pictures of you skiing down to the timberline," he told his companions.

That was the last time that anyone saw Jim Carter.

Bob Lee, a well-known Portland mountaineer, was a member of the Seattle Mountain Search and Rescue Unit at the time. He was later a leader of the 1961 American Himalayan Expedition and adviser to the 1963 American expedition.

Lee is no stranger to remote mountain areas, but he describes the search for Jim Carter as "the most eerie experience I have ever had." He adds, "Whenever I was away from the rest of the search party, I felt that something or somebody was watching me. There were times when I know the hair on my neck was standing straight up. It was incredibly eerie. I was unarmed except for my ice ax and, believe me, I never let go of that."

Lee was one of the first searchers to reach Carter's ski tracks. A discarded film box lay at the point where he had taken his photos of the Seattle group skiing down to the timberline. From that point on, the tracks in the snow told a part of the story. But only a part.

"Carter evidently took off down the mountain in a wild, death-defying dash, taking chances that no skier of his caliber would take unless something was terribly wrong or he was being pursued," says Lee. "He jumped over two or three large crevasses and was obviously going like the devil."

When Carter's tracks reached the nearly straight-up-and-down sides of Ape Canyon, the searchers were amazed to see that the skier had gone right down the canyon wall. Members of the Mountain Search and Rescue Unit knew that no man on earth could ski down an incline like that and live to tell the story. But when the men climbed down to the bottom of the canyon to retrieve Carter's smashed body, they were unable to find a thing.

The search went on for two weeks. Sometimes there

were as many as seventy-five people in the search party, yet no sign of Carter, his skis, or his equipment was ever found. The complete disappearance of Jim Carter is an unsolved mystery to this day.

Bob Lee and others from the Mountain Search and Rescue Unit, however, have their own theory. Carter was not the type to commit suicide. He was a healthy and wholesome young man who loved the out-of-doors. Something had frightened him out of his wits or he wouldn't have come tearing down the mountain like a madman. Perhaps he was looking over his shoulder at his pursuer and shot off into Ape Canyon before he could stop. Or perhaps he was so terrified that he was willing to take any risk—no matter how great—to get away from whatever it was that was pursuing him.

"Several of us came to the conclusion that the apes got Carter," says Lee. "It seems to be the only explanation."

Probably it is. After studying the tracks, the men could tell almost exactly where Carter would have landed in the canyon. Yet a two weeks' search with as many as seventy-five men taking part produced nothing.

There are several apparently endless caves in and near Ape Canyon and they're appropriately called Ape Caves. They're virtually unexplored because few people care to go near them. It's reasonable to assume, then, that the giant creature—or creatures—carried their victim and his equipment to one of the caves.

It may not be a happy thought, but it seems to be the only answer.

17

For some reason, it makes us rather sad to think that Bigfoot might be a killer and perhaps even a cannibal. We would like to think that our giants are friendly and playful. It's amusing to hear of them hurling culverts, drums of diesel fuel, and tires into a ravine. We can even laugh when they steal someone's deer or shake someone up in his car. It's very different, though, when we hear of them behaving badly.

Actually, there are comparatively few instances on record of Bigfoot misbehaving, and some of them are worth thinking about. We already know that Bigfoot may have had a reason for killing Bauman's partner. If Bauman had, after all, wounded him, then Bigfoot was simply protecting himself from men with guns.

Why poor old Albert Ostman was kidnapped, we don't know. Did the sasquatches want him for their Sunday dinner or did they want to keep him around as a sort of pet? Ostman admits that he was never mistreated. He says, too, that the sasquatches gave him grass with long, sweet roots to eat, and perhaps they thought that was what he always ate. Of course, if the sasquatches had been planning to have Ostman for dinner, that's a horse of a different color.

In most cases it appears that Bigfoot's curiosity is his dangerous and fatal flaw. It's quite possible that he watched the skiers out of curiosity. It's even possible that he was trying to race Carter down to the timberline. Or he may have seen Carter taking photographs and walked up for a better look. It's not too farfetched to assume, then, that it was also curiosity that prompted Bigfoot to carry Carter and his equipment off to a cave.

Bigfoot's curiosity is a pretty well established fact. On one occasion a truck driver was driving slowly along a lonely road deep in the wilderness. All at once he let out a squeal of fright. A huge man about seven or eight feet tall and all covered with hair was running alongside the truck and peering through the window at the driver. The unfortunate man lost control of both himself and his vehicle and they shot off the road and into a tree. The truck was rather badly damaged, but was that Bigfoot's fault?

It wouldn't be nice to blame Bigfoot for another incident that happened on the slopes of Mount Saint Helens, either. A troop of boy scouts from Centralia, Washington, had come up the mountain with their scoutmaster for a camp-out. All went well the first day. The boys pitched their tents, fished, cooked, studied nature, and did all the other things that boy scouts do.

On the afternoon of the second day, a group of them decided to go exploring. It turned out to be an afternoon that the boys will always remember. Although the sun was shining, the forest was rather dark and gloomy. They were walking along an old logging trail. The branches of the trees came together overhead and it was somewhat like walking through a tunnel.

It was a pleasant and exciting experience for the boys. Birds were chirping, and they saw squirrels, chipmunks, and a deer. Then they saw something else!

They saw Bigfoot! He was coming along the logging trail toward them. The boys stood rooted to the spot, their eyes bugging out in terror. There was nothing in their Scout Manual to tell them what to do if they met a huge hairy giant in the forest, so they did the sensible thing: they turned around and streaked back to camp as fast as they could go.

Several of the boys were in a state of complete hysterics when they reached camp. Some thought the hairy giant was about to attack them. Others were sure that it had chased them for over a mile. All agreed that "it was at least fourteen feet high and looked just like a great, big, huge gorilla."

The scoutmaster sighed. The boys were in such an upset state that he knew he couldn't keep them on the mountain any longer. Besides, he wasn't too happy about being up there himself. Camp was struck quickly and the boy scouts from Centralia hurried home to tell their hair-raising story.

Once again, Bigfoot made the headlines.

18

Bigfoot not only captured occasional national headlines but also managed to become the star of his own publication.

It was probably a whim more than anything else that prompted George Haas of Oakland, California, to put out the *Bigfoot Bulletin*. After retiring, George had plenty of time to read. He gobbled up everything he could on science fiction first, then he became interested in the study of unexplained things that are ignored by scientists rather than investigated by them. This, of course, led him straight into the long, hairy arms of Bigfoot.

The *Bulletin* was a tremendous boon to the researchers. Up until that time, there had been almost no means of communication. A few kept in fairly regular contact by mail, and that was about it. John Green, away off up in British Columbia, felt rather left out of things. If it hadn't been for men like Jim McClarin, he wouldn't even have known what was going on in Humboldt County, where so much of the action was taking place.

A lot of the researchers' problems were solved by the *Bigfoot Bulletin*. Reports of footprints and sightings were listed, and those interested now knew what was taking place in other parts of the Bigfoot world. Nobody was able to read all the newspapers and magazines, but the *Bulletin* tried to list every article in any publication that mentioned the hairy giant.

The very first issue had an article by Jim McClarin based on an article that had been published by the *Crescent City News* in 1896 and might be the oldest written account of the sighting of a Bigfoot in northern California. There were many reported sightings before that time, but as far as anyone knows they were never printed.

McClarin's article told about an explorer who had seen a "huge, hairy Wild Man" in Siskiyou County, California. The wild man was standing about 150 yards from the explorer and was pulling leaves or tender shoots off some bushes. It was of gigantic size, at least seven feet tall, and very broad across the shoulders. It made a screaming sound and its voice was like that of a woman in great fear. The explorer aimed his gun at the creature several times, but couldn't shoot because it seemed so human. He later learned that other people had also seen the "huge, hairy Wild Man." All agreed in their descriptions, except that some insisted it was much more than seven feet tall.

The publisher of the *Bigfoot Bulletin* was amazed at the success of his modest little publication. Letters poured in from all over the place and the *Bulletin* got larger and larger as more and more people volunteered information. One issue contained reports of six sightings that Haas considered believable enough to be published. He could never guarantee the accuracy of the reports received, but he tried his best to weed out those that sounded even remotely suspicious.

Before long George Haas found himself the busiest retired man in California. The trickle of mail had become a flood. People from all over the United States, Canada, and Europe wrote to him for further information on Bigfoot. Nearly all of them also wanted to receive copies of the *Bulletin*. George dutifully answered all letters that he received from people he thought were sincere, and every month more copies of the *Bigfoot Bulletin* went into the mail. Not a penny was charged for the *Bulletin* and the publisher soon learned that the pile of correspondence was costing him a pile of money for paper and postage.

Two years after its birth, the *Bigfoot Bulletin* died a sudden death. It wasn't because George Haas had found it too expensive or too time-consuming. It ceased to exist because the publisher had decided to go up to northern California and try to find Bigfoot himself.

19

Willow Creek, California, is really not much more than a wide spot on Highway 299. During the Gold Rush days, it was known as China Flat and was a distributing point for the numerous gold-mining camps in the area. Gold panning is still a popular and sometimes profitable pastime, but timber is the major industry today.

California is a very large state and little Willow Creek boasts a population of just over one thousand. It's tucked away in the heart of the largest forest of Douglas fir in the world. Although the village is quite a distance from anywhere, everyone in the state knows where it is. Why? Because Willow Creek calls itself "The Gateway to Bigfoot Country."

Bigfoot is rapidly becoming big business in little Willow Creek. Tourists eagerly buy Bigfoot postcards and "lifelike" statuettes of the hairy giant. There's a Bigfoot Dance Club, and something is always going on at the Bigfoot Golf and Country Club. Each Labor Day weekend, a celebration is held in honor of Bigfoot.

Bigfoot Daze, as the celebration is appropriately called, begins with a Bigfoot breakfast. The crowning of the Bigfoot Queen follows, and after that the residents and visitors get down to some serious fun. The three-day program includes a whiskerino contest in which all bearded men are judged, go-cart races, a barbecue followed by a Bigfoot Dance, a frog-jumping contest, and a host of other events.

Willow Creek is only a short distance from Bluff Creek, where Bigfoot almost stopped Ray Wallace's road-building project in 1958. Most of the men in the area are enthusiastic outdoorsmen. They spend a lot of time hunting and fishing, and quite a few of them have seen the giant footprints and some have seen Bigfoot himself. Not everyone is a believer, of course, but there are sensible and intelligent men like Al Hodgson, owner of the Willow Creek Variety Store, Syl McCoy, a forestry officer, and many others who are absolutely convinced that strange, hairy giants are roaming around in the nearby forests.

The believers are quick to tell you that Bigfoot is no stranger to the Willow Creek region. Indians on the Hoopa Reservation say that their people have always known about the tribe of big people who lived in the hills. As early as the 1880s, explorers and prospectors told about huge, manlike creatures they had seen during the course of their wanderings. Reports said that the creatures were usually seen between Happy Camp and Willow Creek. They were seven to eight feet tall and weighed between 350 and 800 pounds. They had high, shrill voices, slanted foreheads, broad wide nostrils, short ears, and bodies completely covered with hair.

The same description of Bigfoot seems to apply today.

20

When you enter Willow Creek on Highway 299 coming from the west, the first thing you see is a huge statue of Bigfoot. It's carved from the trunk of a redwood tree and is Jim McClarin's gift to the community.

Jim McClarin is a tall, handsome young man who caught Bigfoot fever in a big way. He became so obsessed with the idea of capturing one of the creatures that he dropped out of Humboldt State College in his senior year so that he could devote all his time to his new interest. Using every cent of his savings and all the money he could borrow, he financed and led a small expedition into the Bluff Creek area. The fact that the expedition was unsuccessful only made Jim more determined than ever.

A host of enormous problems faced Jim, but he had no intentions of giving up. First, he had no money and no one seemed interested in contributing to his Bigfoot Fund, Inc. Second, the Department of Fish and Game informed him that if he did manage to capture Bigfoot, they would confiscate the creature. Third, Jim planned to use tranquilizers and nets to capture Bigfoot. Nobody could tell him, though, which drugs to use because nobody was sure whether Bigfoot was an animal or a human. This meant, then, that the creature might be killed if the wrong drug was used. If that happened and it could be proved that Bigfoot was a human being, McClarin would have to face a murder charge. Fourth, if McClarin captured Bigfoot and put him on display to make money, he would really find himself in trouble if the creature turned out to be human. This would be a violation of California's Little Lindbergh Law, which is punishable by death. Last, if he brought one in and turned it over to an organization for scientific study, he would have to face kidnapping charges if the scientists decided that Bigfoot was a human being.

McClarin must have felt that the whole state of California was trying to keep him from capturing Bigfoot. Even an editorial in the *Humboldt Standard* asking that Bigfoot be protected by law seemed to be aimed at him.

The editorial writer suggested that the state legislature pass a bill "legalizing Bigfoot." This elusive nature-child of the wilderness has harmed no one, he wrote, and it has done much for the publicity so important to tourism. And who at this time is to say that Bigfoot, if he and his tribe exist, is not a human being? Primordial, perhaps, but human. Any person bringing in a dead Bigfoot may find himself facing a charge of homicide.

We ask the legislators in the January session, the editorial continued, to take action to make Bigfoot an honorary citizen of California, protected by all its laws, with the dignity and rights that should be his to enjoy.

When George Haas, former editor of the now defunct *Bigfoot Bulletin,* made some inquiries, he learned that Bigfoot was already fully protected by law.

Mr. B. E. Faist, chief of the Wildlife Protection Branch, told him, "We're not concerned with the existence or nonexistence of Bigfoot, but I assure you that the current California fish and game laws or penal code sections do fully protect this animal if such a creature does exist.

"First, any person who kills this alleged creature would be in violation of California fish and game laws if Bigfoot is classified as an animal. Any taking of animals is prohibited in California unless such taking is authorized in the California Fish and Game Code or California Fish and Game Commission regulations. There is no provision for the capture of Bigfoot in any of our fish and game laws.

"Second, any person who kills this alleged creature would be prosecuted for murder under appropriate sections of the California Penal Code if Bigfoot is determined to be human."

All of this must have come as a great relief to Bigfoot, but it didn't cheer Jim McClarin up one little bit. This is certainly understandable. Jim had been a zoology major at Humboldt State College and his interest in the creature was purely scientific. "If I do capture Bigfoot, I'll take him to the Fleischhacker Zoo in San Francisco," he says. "He won't be put on display. He'll be kept there for his own protection and so that scientists can study him. After the scientific studies have been completed, he'll be taken back to where he came from."

Over the years, Jim has unselfishly done whatever he could to assist other Bigfoot researchers whom he considered reliable. He has worked closely with John Green in British Columbia, keeping him informed of any new developments. He also contributed articles regularly to the *Bigfoot Bulletin*.

Most of the time, however, is spent trying to organize expeditions. Although Jim feels strongly that Bigfoot belongs to the same family as man, he's not really concerned about any possible consequences. He's not going to kill the creature, so he won't face a murder charge. He's not planning to put him on display for profit, so the courts couldn't sentence him to death under California's Little Lindbergh Law.

As far as any other laws are concerned, McClarin won't worry about them until after he's captured Bigfoot and smuggled him to San Francisco.

Most people wish Jim McClarin the very best of luck. He's never been afraid to stand up and tell the world that he believes in Bigfoot. A few people, of course, think that he's a crackpot. Jim is still going strong, though, and nobody has yet suggested that he be put away on a funny farm.

21

The *San Francisco Chronicle* published a series of articles on Bigfoot in December, 1965, because "there is mounting testimony that giant man-animals may be roaming the remote forests and mountains of the northwestern part of the United States."

The following article appeared in the December 7, 1965, issue:

THEY SAW THE MAN-ANIMAL
By George Draper

The belief that several hundred giant man-animals are roaming the wilderness areas of California, Oregon and Washington was expressed yesterday by the owner of a Fresno lock and safe company.

"There is absolutely no doubt in my mind that they exist," said O. R. Edwards, "and I know they are extremely strong and very intelligent."

Edwards, 56, a legitimate safe cracker with an uncanny knack for twirling the dials of the most formidable strong box, also believes these man-animals are "extremely dangerous" and "capable of mutilating a human being."

"I wouldn't be here today if I'd shot at those I saw," he said with disarming frankness.

Edwards is one of a dozen or more people who claim to have had face-to-face encounters with the hair-covered giants that they say stand between seven and 10 feet tall and weigh more than 500 pounds.

Another terrifying face-to-face encounter with a man-animal has been reported by Don L. Hunter, head of the Audio-Visual Department at the University of Oregon.

Hunter caught a glimpse of a giant taking enormous strides across a meadow at Todd Lake in the rugged Three Sisters Wilderness Area of Central Oregon.

"Even now the back of my neck gets all cold when I think about it," Hunter said while sitting in his comfortable home on a hill overlooking Eugene.

The University official said he and his former wife, who was with him and who also saw the creature, became so petrified that they spent the night in their car after driving 10 miles away from the scene.

Hunter said he has been trained in the scientific method of testing everything he sees and hears.

"I can't believe it was an hallucination. Two of us saw it. My wife was just as scared as I was," he said.

Edwards, who said "he was raised in the woods and used to be a good mountain man" was hunting with his friend, Bill Cole, when he encountered a man-animal in the southern Siskiyou Mountains during World War II.

This is Edwards' account of the meeting:

"We were both moving slowly and silently around this patch of brush. Bill went around the left side; I went around the right.

"I was sweeping the area ahead with my eyes. On one sweep, I caught a glimpse of what seemed like an apelike head sticking out of the brush.

"Dashing back to the end of the brush I saw a large manlike creature covered with brown hair. It was about seven feet tall and carrying in its arms what seemed like a man. "I could only see legs and shoes. It was heading straight downhill on the run.

"I was about 30 feet away and the opening in the brush was only 10–15 feet wide. At the speed he was going it didn't leave me much time to make observations.

"I, of course, did not believe what I had just seen. So I closed my eyes and shook my head to sort of clear things up.

"I looked down the hill again in time to see the back and shoulders and head of a manlike thing covered with brown hair. It was disappearing into the brush some 70 or 80 yards below."

To confirm his recollections of what happened that day, Edwards wrote a letter to Cole at Grand Island, Nebraska, last year.

"I guess I should have started looking for you. I don't know why, but I didn't," Edwards wrote. "Maybe I was afraid of the creature. Maybe I was afraid I'd find you dead."

Cole replied, acknowledging the incident, but saying, "I don't think it carried me at all. I was conscious all the time. I didn't hurt any place."

Cole said that after he "quit rolling," he went back up the hill and got his rifle. "I stood there some time and just looked and listened. I had a feeling I was being watched and hunted," Cole added in his letter.

Sitting in the back room of his Fresno lock and safe shop, Edwards says he has heard many stories about the Bigfoot giants from men who claim to have seen them.

"But Cole," he said, "is the only man I know who has had physical contact with a giant."

Edwards mentioned one other thing in his letter to Cole—that for 20 years "I would not believe what I had seen."

And to this Cole replied:

"Funny, neither of us has the guts to say what happened to us."

Prior to the exchange of these letters, it would

seem, Edwards and Cole never discussed what took place on that unusual day.

Edwards also said he saw two more man-animals in the brush at the bottom of the ravine as he worked his way back to the logging road where their car was parked.

"Then came the darndest whistling scream that I ever heard from right behind me," he said.

"My hackles went up as I whirled around just in time to see a flash of something brown disappear behind the tree."

Other observers have described the man-animal's strange cry as "a vibrating sound" or like the sound of a steam locomotive's whistle or the sound of metal tearing.

"All I can say is that it's one of the weirdest sounds I ever heard in my life—a vibrating wail, like a person in great pain," said R. A. E. Morley, a geologist.

Morley, who believes it was a giant that hurled a boulder at him while he was swimming in a mountain stream, said he heard the man-animal scream one night in the Siskiyous southwest of Grants Pass.

The sound unnerved and completely deranged his dog, Morley said, and caused the animal to froth at the mouth and hide under the cabin mat.

22

The human mind can play very strange tricks on a person. Don Hunter said he couldn't believe that what he had seen was an hallucination. Then he quickly added that his wife had also seen it and was just as scared as he was. If Hunter had been alone, he probably would have convinced himself that he hadn't actually seen what he saw. There ain't no such animal, he might have thought, therefore I couldn't possibly have seen it.

A few points in the story that O. R. Edwards told the reporter need some clarifying. Edwards apparently abandoned Cole. He saw the giant manlike creature run off with his partner, but he says that he couldn't believe what he had just seen. At any rate, he made no effort to rescue Cole. He worked his way back to the logging road where their car was parked and drove home alone.

We can't be too hard on Edwards. He was frightened out of his wits and probably in a state of shock. He had seen something happen that no other man had ever seen. It was something too incredible to be true. In his letter to Cole, Edwards says that for twenty years he would not believe what he had seen. He admits that he should have started looking for him, then adds that perhaps he didn't because he was afraid of the creature or that he was afraid that he would find his partner dead. The fact that Edwards made no effort to rescue Cole can be forgiven. He was in such a state that he can hardly be blamed for running off. Whether or not his conscience bothered him for deserting his partner isn't known.

Cole, on the other hand, said, "I don't think it carried me at all. I was conscious all the time. I didn't hurt any place."

A particularly frightening experience is sometimes hidden away in the back of a person's mind. This must have been true in Cole's case. He had been carried off by a hairy giant, then for some unknown reason tossed aside as the creature raced down a hill. It was an experience so terrifying that some secret mechanism made him forget that it had ever happened. It wasn't until he received Edwards's letter twenty years later that the secret mechanism was unlocked and the incident again came to his mind.

For twenty long years, neither Cole nor Edwards told their story to one another. Neither of them, it seems, believed what he had seen and what had happened. If Edwards had not written to Cole, their story would never have been told.

The publicity given to Bigfoot brought out another story of a man who had met the hairy giant. The man had been driving for hours and pulled off the road in a lonely stretch of forest to stretch his legs. It was after midnight and the sky was overcast. He was sitting on the fender of his car when he heard someone walking down the road. Curious as to who would be walking through a lonely mountain area at that time of the night, he got into the car and turned on the lights. Then he got the fright of his life! He saw, coming toward him, what he at first thought was a big bear walking on its hind legs. He then put his lights on bright and the thing looked like a human in an ape costume, but was much too large for that. "I swear I never saw anything so big in my life," the man declared. "It stood there a couple of minutes more, then jumped off the road. I was so scared that I just sat there and shook for an hour.

"I vowed that I would never say anything about that night and couldn't believe that I really saw something so ugly. I was honestly afraid that I had lost my mind."

Such vows of silence in regard to Bigfoot sightings are a common phenomenon. John Green believes that many sightings are not reported simply because people are afraid of ridicule. It often happens, too, that those who do report sightings ask that their names not be mentioned.

It's unfortunately true that a person who says that he's seen Bigfoot is often inviting ridicule. One Washington couple almost got a divorce because the husband had made a fool of himself by telling the local newspaper that he'd seen the creature while fishing in the Lewis River. A responsible and competent geologist for an oil company was very nearly fired because he reported a sighting. His boss told him that this was evidence of "diminished responsibility."

In plain words, the boss was telling the young geologist that he had rocks in his head.

The rugged terrain of the Pacific Northwest is an ideal habitat for Bigfoot. This is Mount Saint Helens in the state of Washington. Courtesy of the Washington State Travel Development Division.

John Green's map of Bigfoot sightings and track reports in the United States and Canada as chronicled in his book *The Sasquatch File* copyright © 1973 by John Green, published by Cheam Publishing Ltd., Box 99, Agassiz, British Columbia, Canada. The number of reports indicated in each area is not complete, but gives some idea of the geographical range of Bigfoot. Courtesy of John Green.

A painting of Bigfoot made from a blowup of a frame of the Patterson film of Bigfoot. The facial detail is accurate according to a close study of the blowup. Courtesy of Ron Olson of North American Wildlife Research Association.

A clip from Patterson's famous film of Bigfoot. Courtesy of
Ron Olson of North American Wildlife Research Association.

John Green, Canada's foremost Bigfoot (Sasquatch) researcher, with his collection of casts of Bigfoot prints.

Ron Olson of North American Wildlife Research sporting the normal equipment required for a Bigfoot expedition—a tranquilizing gun, a camera, and a side arm. Courtesy of Ron Olson.

23

One of the letters received by Roger Patterson, a Bigfoot enthusiast from Yahima, Washington, was along the same lines as the story of Cole and Edwards. The man's story rang true in every way, yet the man himself couldn't swear that it was true. The letter intrigued Patterson. He wasn't sure what to think about it, however, and he sent it to John Green for his opinion. Green was so fascinated that he drove down to Washington State to talk to the man.

It was an interesting but confusing interview. The experience had been such a shock that the man's mind refused to accept it as something that really had happened to him. He forgot all about the horrifying experience until he started reading the articles about Bigfoot.

John Green must have felt that there was some truth to the story because he gave many of the details in his book *The Sasquatch File*. Because the man thought that his mind might be playing tricks on him, he asked that he be known only as Bill.

In 1952 Bill and two other men, named Lee Vlery and Josh Russell, went to Orleans, near Willow Creek, California, to start preliminary work on a logging operation. One evening Josh told Bill that Lee had gone up to Happy Camp earlier with someone else. He wouldn't have any transportation back and he wanted Bill to pick him up there. Bill went, but he wasn't too happy about it. The rain was coming down in buckets and the road through the mountains was extremely crooked and dangerous. Bill was even less happy when he got to Happy Camp and was told that Lee had gotten a lift back to Orleans with another logger.

It was raining harder than ever when he began the return trip. Just a few miles outside of Happy Camp, he was flagged down by someone with a flashlight. The man told him that there had been a landslide and the road was closed. He said, though, that Bill could still get back to Orleans by way of a detour across the Eel River. It was a dirt road that went through Bear Valley and came out at the mouth of Bluff Creek a few miles below Orleans.

About twenty miles down the road, Bill saw a strange creature all covered with shaggy, bluish gray hair. Now what in the world can that be? he asked himself. A gorilla or an ogre or what? An instant later, the thing stepped back into the forest. Bill shrugged his shoulders and drove on, quite certain that he had only imagined seeing some unexplainable something.

Suddenly, with no warning and for no reason at all, his car went into a violent skid. Bill fought desperately for control. The muddy road followed along the side of a canyon, and to go over the edge meant almost certain death. When he got his car under control, he happened to glance into the rearview mirror and thought he saw an ugly face peering at him through the back window. The face disappeared and Bill again concluded that he had only been imagining things.

About a quarter of a mile farther on, a small six-inch sapling had fallen across the road. Bill stopped the car, got out, and tried to pull it off to one side.

Before he managed to move it, he heard the sound of running feet thudding toward him. He knew at once what it was! The feet belonged to the hairy creature he had seen in his headlights and peering through his rear window.

Whatever the thing was, it wasn't friendly. It kept circling around the driver in a most menacing manner. The mouth was open in an angry snarl and Bill saw that its eye teeth were much longer than a human's. The head was set squarely on the shoulders and the hair on the head was shorter than the hair on the body. The creature was no more than six feet tall, but it was very heavily and powerfully built.

After a few minutes of circling and snarling, the thing changed its tactics. It would stalk off down the road, then come charging back when the driver started for his car. It was becoming more and more menacing. The cat-and-mouse game may have been fun for Bigfoot, but Bill was paralyzed by fear. The creature could seize him at any moment. He knew that he had to get out of there—and fast!

Bill suddenly made a desperate bid for escape. He made it with only a split second to spare. The door had just slammed shut when Bigfoot was there trying to claw his way through the window. The driver jerked the car into gear, stamped on the accelerator, and smashed his way through the sapling. Bigfoot let out a scream of rage and frustration "like the scream of a stallion and the roar of a mad grizzly" when his victim—or playmate—made his escape.

Almost as incredible as Bill's experience is the fact that he promptly forgot all about it. The whole matter simply went out of his mind and he remembered nothing of what happened.

This is even more amazing in view of what took

place the next day when he talked to Lee Vlery, who had come home the same way just an hour or so before Bill. Vlery asked him if he had noticed anything unusual on the road, and Bill replied that he hadn't. Vlery then told him that a great hairy thing that looked almost like a man had tried to push their car off the road. Then he added that there was something awfully strange going on around the Bluff Creek area.

Later that same day, Vlery noticed that Bill's car had a large dent in the front and asked what had happened. Bill had absolutely no recollection of crashing his way through the sapling and told Vlery he didn't know how the dent got there.

When talking to John Green, Bill said, "The story finally came sneaking out of my subconscious. I remembered more and more details about that horrible night and, believe me, I had a bad case of the jitters."

And it's not hard to understand why.

24

The series of articles about California's Abominable Snowman in the *San Francisco Chronicle* jogged many memories. Not only did it bring in a flurry of letters from people who claimed that they had seen the monster man-animal that roams the Pacific Northwest wilderness, it also brought in a set of rather fuzzy photographs. If authentic, said the accompanying article, the photographs would be the only ones ever taken of the hulking apelike creature whose hideous screams had terrorized outdoorsmen from California's central Sierra to the forests of Washington.

Dick Russell, assistant manager of Brooks Cameras in San Francisco, brought the pictures to the *Chronicle*. A grizzled old woodsman named Zack Hamilton had left the roll of film at the camera shop to be processed. He told Russell that he had just come in from the Three Sisters wilderness area in Oregon, where he had been stalked by a hairy monster. He wasn't sure, but he thought he might have gotten some photographs of the creature with his cheap little camera.

The film remained in the files for three years and one day Russell took the pictures out and examined them. "I got prickly all over when I realized they were the pictures the old-timer said he had taken in the brush," Russell told the *Chronicle*. "I've never seen anything like them. After studying the photos, I put them back in the file because they didn't belong to us."

When Russell read the series of articles in the *Chronicle* about the search for Bigfoot, he was reminded of the old woodsman's eerie tale and the unclaimed film that was still in the files. It had now been five years since Zack Hamilton had left the film for processing. "If he hasn't claimed them after all this time, I don't think he ever will," said Russell. "He just dropped in out of nowhere. I had never seen him before and I've never seen him since."

The photographers and reporters at the *Chronicle* gasped when Russell showed them the film. The photographs were typical of those taken by an amateur with a cheap camera. They were fuzzy and lacked contrast. Moreover, they had been taken in the middle of a tangled growth of heavy forest and there hadn't been enough light to take really first-class pictures with a camera of that type.

As bad as the photographs were, they created a frenzy of excitement among the *Chronicle* staff. Several shots showed a huge, hulking, apelike or manlike creature. It had long arms and rather short legs and was entirely covered with dark hair. The head seemed to be set squarely upon a pair of massive shoulders. In spite of the poor quality of the photographs, it could easily be seen that the creature was enormous.

The men couldn't decide whether the brute was more closely related to a man or an ape, but all of them did agree on one thing. They all agreed that the photographs were the real thing and not a hoax.

"An old woodsman couldn't possibly fake a thing like that," Dick Russell said earnestly.

And that's how it happened that camera-shy Bigfoot got his picture in a large metropolitan newspaper.

25

Not long after Bigfoot had received all the publicity in the *San Francisco Chronicle*, he made big news in the Washington papers. A man near Yakima bumped into him in an apple orchard and came very close to having a heart attack. He was frightened so badly, in fact, that he had to be taken to the hospital and treated for shock.

Completely unrepentant, Bigfoot pulled another one of his naughty tricks soon afterward in the same area. A young man was driving toward Yakima about eleven o'clock one night. Rain was pouring down and sheets of lightning seemed to be flashing everywhere. Visibility was poor and the young man proceeded cautiously in the driving rain. Suddenly a huge form loomed straight up in front of him. It was standing right in the middle of the road. The young man slammed on the brakes and skidded to a halt, stopping only about three feet from the creature. The hairy giant just stood there and looked down at the driver. This did very little for the driver's peace of mind. He had killed the engine of his car when he slammed on the brakes and now he couldn't get it started again.

Either Bigfoot was his usual curious self that stormy night or else he was in a playful mood. In two giant strides he reached the back of the car and looked through the rear window. He then walked over to the driver's side, bent down, and peered straight into the face of the young man, who was trying desperately to get his car started. It was a nasty night and here he was stalled on a lonely road ten miles from town. Being out there alone with Mr. Bigfoot was just about the last thing in the world that he wanted.

The face peering through the window of the car was not a very pretty one. The nose was flat and wide and looked rather like that of a person who had had his nose squashed. Grayish white hair covered the entire creature except for the lips and just around the eyes. The driver, though, didn't get a good look at its hands or feet.

When Bigfoot stood in the headlights of the car, its

eyes glowed "sort of like a rabbit's or something when you shine a light in them at night." The young man, however, didn't notice anything particularly unusual about the eyes while the creature was peering at him through the window. "I guess I was too busy trying to get my car started," he explained.

His other observations, though, fit in well with other descriptions of Bigfoot. The lips were thin, but the jaw was large and heavy and appeared to stick out farther then the nose. The eye teeth were more prominent than the front teeth. They weren't fangs, but they slanted forward and out. The forehead was very low, and "the whole face was slanted an awful lot."

The driver estimated the creature's height to be well over seven feet. It had the shape of a man but was much, much heavier and very much broader. It was obviously a very powerful beast that could have tipped the car over easily. Fortunately Bigfoot was merely curious. He was quite happy to peer at the strange creature inside and he never even touched the car. Neither did he add to the driver's fright by letting out one of his piercing screams.

Everything considered, Bigfoot was remarkably well behaved that night. He was standing in the middle of the road, it's true, but that's probably not against the law. And when the young man finally got his car started and got out of there as fast as he could, Bigfoot was still standing in the middle of the road. Perhaps he was lonely and was hoping that someone else would stop and visit with him for a while.

26

A logger in Oregon had the highly unusual experience of watching a Bigfoot family having lunch. He allowed John Green to put his story on tape, but asked him not to use his name. "I don't want people to think I'm some kind of a nut," he explained logically.

It was bitterly cold on the day the incident took place. Fog blanketed the valley and an icy wind was blowing. The elevation was somewhere between 4,000 and 5,000 feet above sea level.

The man was walking along a mountain trail when he noticed some large, flat rocks that had recently been turned over. The fog had covered all the other rocks with a film of moisture, but these were dry. That's strange, he thought. Why would anyone want to do that?

Then he saw something stranger! Three creatures were busily doing something or other on a nearby ridge of rocks. They looked almost like humans except that they were covered with fur or hair from top to bottom. The astonished logger suddenly realized that he was watching a Bigfoot family. There was Papa Bigfoot, Mama Bigfoot, and Baby Bigfoot.

The ridge was about fifty feet higher than the clump of bushes the logger was hiding in, but he still had a fairly good view. He couldn't imagine, though, what the creatures were doing. Papa and Mama were in a stooped or squatting position. They kept moving along slowly, picking up one large rock after another, sniffing them, and them putting them aside.

After a few minutes of this, Papa Bigfoot must have found what he was looking for and he really went into action. Rocks weighing fifty, sixty, or even one hundred pounds were jerked out and stacked up. The hole got deeper and deeper and the stacks of rocks got higher and higher. The logger noticed that some of the stacks of large, flat rocks were piled in such a way that they could have fallen on Papa Bigfoot. This didn't seem to bother him, however. He kept jerking the rocks out and stacking them up on shaky piles.

At long last, the old man found what he wanted. When he crawled out of the hole, he had a large nest of grass in his hands. All the family pawed through the nest and brought out a number of hibernating rodents. They ate them as a boy eats bananas. Mama and Papa got two or three rodents each. Baby Bigfoot had found only one and he seemed to have trouble eating it. He was still tugging and chewing away on his lunch long after his parents had finished theirs.

Papa had started a search for more rodents when he scrambled suddenly to his feet, looked toward the clump of bushes in which the logger was hiding, then made a short, quick dash into the forest. Mama was right on his heels, and the logger thought that she ran holding Baby Bigfoot in front of her. A few seconds later, they disappeared from sight.

The logger told John Green that he was no good at judging height and weight and giving descriptions. He estimated, however, that Papa Bigfoot was well over six feet high and a head taller than his wife. Baby Bigfoot didn't even come up to his mother's hip and was probably only a couple of months old. Both Papa and Mama were extremely heavily built and must have weighed at least several hundred pounds. The old man had demonstrated his strength by effortlessly lifting heavy rocks out of the hole and piling them up above him.

The male was a dirty brown color and his mate was fawn-colored or about the color of buckskin. The only time the man got a good look at their faces was when they had gotten his scent and turned in his direction. He thought their faces somewhat resembled a cat's face, except that he couldn't see any ears. The nose was flat and broad and didn't stick out as a human's does. The upper lip looked short and thin and the forehead sloped backward.

Like so many others who have seen Bigfoot, the logger said, "I just couldn't believe what I was seeing. It just couldn't be true, yet I knew that it was."

John Green is a systematic man who investigates every serious report as thoroughly as possible. He accompanied the logger to the spot where he had seen the three Bigfoot—or sasquatches, as Green has to call them because he's a Canadian—and they found the pile of rocks to which he had referred. The hole dug by the male Bigfoot was about five feet deep and almost as steep-sided as a well. No creature without hands could have lifted the rocks out and piled them up like that, Green concluded.

In two hours of marching around on the mountain, the men found numerous other holes and piles of rocks. "Personally," wrote John Green in his first book, *On the Track of the Sasquatch*, "I'm quite satisfied that these rocks were left piled by Sasquatches that picked them up and sniffed them in a search for hibernating rodents."

Poor Bigfoot, it seems, really has to work hard to find a square meal.

27

In December, 1959, an article by Ivan Sanderson entitled "The Strange Story of America's Abominable Snowman" appeared in *True* magazine. A young man in Yakima, Washington, by the name of Roger Patterson, read the article, and it changed his whole life. It may also have made life somewhat more difficult for Bigfoot.

Patterson, mentioned earlier as the recipient of the letter from Bill, was a former boxer and radeo rider who was making a shaky living as an inventor and promoter when he read Sanderson's article. He couldn't get Bigfoot out of his mind, but it wasn't until five years later that he began spending all his time and money on the search for America's Abominable Snowman. The search went on almost without interruption from 1964 until his death at a relatively early age in 1972.

Willow Creek, California, the Gateway to Bigfoot Country, was the first stop for Patterson and his companion, Rod Thornton. While there, they talked to Al Hodgson, who is one of the local Bigfoot investigators, and to Jerry Crew, the bulldozer operator who had made the first plaster-of-Paris casts of the giant footprints.

Bigfoot hunters by the dozens had stopped in Willow Creek since Sanderson's story had appeared in *True*. Most of them wanted to talk to Hodgson and Crew, and the two men must have been rather tired of answering hundreds of questions. They were impressed by Patterson's sincerity, however, and told him that there had been some fairly recent sightings in the Bluff Creek area. That was the best place to start looking, they believed.

The first man they met at Bluff Creek was Pat Graves. Pat was a timber surveyor for the Forest Service. His work took him deep into the wilderness and he spent much of his time thirty or forty miles from the nearest logging road. There was so much tangled brush in the mountainous terrain, he told them, that a man could hardly fight his way through.

The timber surveyor was a firm believer in Bigfoot. He had seen hundreds of the huge footprints and he knew that they were not faked. "The thing that makes those tracks weighs around a thousand pounds," he declared. "It walks upright, takes enormous strides, has a very humanlike foot, and goes up and down steep slopes where a man just can't go." He then said that he had seen tracks just the day before and told Patterson and Thornton where to find them.

The two men found the tracks almost at once. The creature had come down the mountain, crossed a road, stomped around in an old logging landing, then gone over a bank and back into the brush.

Patterson stared in amazement. The prints were seventeen inches long and five inches across the heel. The creature walked with a stride that measured fifty-two inches. It was enormous. There could be absolutely no doubt about that. Each footprint was an inch and a half deep, but Patterson's footprints were just barely visible. Whoever or whatever had made those tracks had been an awfully big boy.

On their way down the mountain that evening, they stopped to talk to a man who was filling the fuel tanks on some logging equipment. The man lived in a small house trailer parked in a clearing and he didn't like it. Five dogs that he had trained to hunt bear were his only company. The only one who ever visited him was Bigfoot.

Something had come by his place the night before, he told Patterson and Thornton. The dogs were yelping in fear and he stepped outside just in time to hear something running off through the woods. When he went to see his dogs, he found them all huddled together and whining like puppies. The dogs would cheerfully attack any bear, so the man knew that it was something else that had frightened his dogs and he had a pretty good idea what that something else was.

"I think I'll quit this job and get out of here," the man declared. "It's just too spooky around here at night to suit me."

Patterson and Thornton spent the night in a small cabin farther down the mountain. They, too, had a visitor that they couldn't see. About three o'clock in the morning, they were awakened by a loud, high-pitched whine that trailed off into a deep growl. Both of them hurried to the window, but it was too dark to see anything. They did, however, hear something heavy moving through the brush. "I don't know whether it was Bigfoot or not," said Patterson. "I do know, though, that it was the weirdest sound that I've ever heard."

Coming from the state of Washington, Patterson had naturally heard about the giant hairy apes on Mount Saint Helens. Skamania County wasn't far out of his way, and he decided to stop there on the trip home and ask a few questions.

It was early in the morning when they stopped in the tiny logging town of Cougar and went into the only café in the place for breakfast. While drinking his second cup of coffee, Patterson asked the waitress whether any giant hairy apes had been seen lately.

"Oh, yeah," the waitress told him. "There's one just across the street right now. He owns the gas station and his name is Herbert Lindner."

Everyone in the café roared with laughter and Patterson joined them. He had already learned that many people still looked upon Bigfoot as a huge joke.

28

At 3:30 P.M. on October 20, 1967, Roger Patterson and Bob Gimlin were traveling on horseback in the Bluff Creek area. They had just rounded a bend when both of them saw a giant manlike creature standing not more than eighty or ninety feet away from them.

Patterson's horse reared straight up in fright and fell over onto its side. A stirrup was flattened nearly completely and his foot was still in it. "My foot hurt, but I couldn't think about it because I was too busy trying to control the horse and get my camera out of the saddlebag," he says. "I got the camera out all right, but I couldn't control the horse anymore and had to let him go."

Holding the 16 mm. movie camera in his hand, Patterson starting running toward the creature, shooting his color film as he went. It was a tough way to shoot a movie. He had to jump over logs and plow through brush, but he had a bit of luck. The whirring of the camera must have aroused the creature's curiosity. All of a sudden, it stopped dead and looked around at Patterson, then broke into a run and disappeared in the forest.

The two men were wildly excited. Never before had anyone been able to shoot movie film of the elusive Bigfoot. The movie had been taken under very poor conditions, however. A man normally doesn't take pictures while leaping over logs and crashing through brush. A camera is supposed to be held as steady as possible. Fortunately, Bigfoot had been quite cooperative. Until it ran off into the woods, it had shuffled along unhurriedly and had even stopped and looked back for a second or two so that Patterson could get its face on the film.

In spite of their eagerness to get the film developed, the two men still had work to do. Hoping to get more movies, they followed the creature's trail through the forest. When they lost it, they returned to the place where they had first seen Bigfoot and did some measuring. The footprints were 17 inches long and 7½ inches across at the widest part. The strides averaged 41 inches until Bigfoot had gotten nervous and started to run. They then lengthened out to a lusty 65 inches, which must be a big stride even for Bigfoot.

The first thing Patterson did after leaving the wil-

derness area was to get his film processed by an expert.
A copy was also made and the original was locked up
in a safe-deposit box where it couldn't be stolen or
damaged.

When Patterson projected his film, he was delighted
with the results. Much of it was hazy and out of focus
because of camera movement, but he was sure that no
one could doubt that the creature in the film was Bigfoot herself. Yes, that's right. *Herself.* The film was of
a lady Bigfoot. A pair of large, hair-covered breasts
could be seen quite clearly in the part of the movie
where she had stopped and turned around to see what
was going on.

Lady Bigfoot was quite a girl. Patterson estimated
her height at slightly more than seven feet and guessed
her weight to be somewhere in the neighborhood of
four hundred pounds. She may have been pretty to a
male Bigfoot, but a human being could not possibly
call her attractive. Brownish hair covered her from top
to bottom. Her head was set squarely upon a pair of
massive shoulders. Her legs were too short and her
arms far too long. Besides, her feet were much too big.

Both Patterson and Gimlin knew that many people
would accuse them of faking the film. Hoping to prevent that, they went to see the special-effects people at
Universal Studios in Hollywood. These are the people
who created things like King Kong and all the horrible great monsters who always grab up a beautiful girl
in one hand and threaten to bite her head off. Faking
was their business, and they would certainly recognize
a fake if they saw one. Patterson asked the experts in
Universal Studios to look at his film and then tell him
whether they would be able to reproduce the same
thing.

The experts studied the movie and solemnly shook

their heads. "No, we couldn't," one finally said. "If you gave us a million bucks, we could try, but we'd have to invent a whole set of new, artificial muscles. We'd also have to find someone large enough to fit into a gorilla skin or something similar and teach him to walk like that."

"It might possibly be done," another added, "but I'd guess that it would be very nearly impossible and it would take an awful lot of time and money."

Patterson smiled happily. He was now ready to shock the scientists by showing them his film of Bigfoot.

29

But it wasn't the scientists who got a shock. It was Roger Patterson. The scientists weren't at all interested in seeing his film. "If you can bring me in a skull or something, I'll be glad to have a look at it," one told him, "but I don't have the time to watch any home movies."

Patterson refused to be discouraged. He returned home and invited John Green to come down from British Columbia. Green flew to Yakima, watched the film, and was highly impressed. He told Patterson and Gimlin that if they came to Vancouver he would arrange for the movie to be reviewed by a group of Canadian scientists.

Green kept his promise to the letter. When Patterson and Gimlin got to Vancouver, they were introduced to about a dozen distinguished zoologists and anthropologists. Most of the men admitted that they had been highly skeptical when they arrived at the meeting, but they had left somewhat shaken. Several of them confessed that although no concrete scientific proof existed, they were now close to being convinced that huge, hairy man-animals were roaming about in the wilderness areas of the Pacific Northwest.

Anthropologist Don Abbott said, "It's about as hard to believe that the film is faked as it is to admit that such a creature really lives. If there's a chance to follow it up scientifically, my curiosity has reached the point where I'd want to go along with it."

Another anthropologist declared, "I'm not one hundred percent convinced, but I think the film is genuine. And if I were out in the mountains and I saw a thing like that, I wouldn't shoot it. I'd be too afraid of how human it would look under the fur."

The report of Patterson's movie got a big play in the press and one of the leading American weeklies invited Roger and Bob Gimlin to come to New York. The editors were interested in seeing the film and wanted to get the straight story from the men who had taken it. As soon as they were settled in their hotel, Patterson called Ivan Sanderson, whose article in *True* magazine had first set him off on his search for Bigfoot.

Sanderson rushed right over. He was one of the very few scientists who actually believed in the existence of Bigfoot and wasn't afraid to say so. After seeing the film, he was convinced beyond a shadow of a doubt that it was genuine. At long last the elusive creature had been captured on film. Sanderson was certain that the movie would be widely acclaimed and promised the men that he would do everything in his power to help them.

Poor Patterson and Gimlin soon learned that they needed help. New York was a strange, cold city to these men from the far West. They were anxious to do what had to be done and then get back home. But one disappointment followed another. The editors of the weekly saw the film and wanted proof that it wasn't faked. Patterson proved this as well as he could and the editors demanded further confirmation. It was impossible for the men to get a straight answer. After being kept in suspense for a week, they were abruptly informed by the editors that the publication was no longer interested in either the film or the story.

A picture magazine then expressed interest and Patterson and Gimlin trotted hopefully over with their film. The editors had arranged to have the film studied by several zoologists and anthropologists and it was duly sent to them. It almost came flying back and the whole thing was dismissed as a colossal hoax.

Ivan Sanderson was furious. The scientists, he believed, had not even taken enough time to study the film carefully. They had simply stated that the existence of such a creature was impossible. And that was it! "Don't worry," he consoled Patterson and Gimlin. "Just give me a few days to see what I can do."

Sanderson swung into swift action and at last things began happening. *Argosy* magazine agreed to cooperate, and so did several leading scientists with distinguished qualifications. They were:

1 / Mr. N. O. Woods, Director of Management Operations for the United States Department of the Interior.

2 / Dr. A. Joseph Wraight, Chief Geographer of the United States Coast and Geodetic Survey.

3 / Dr. John Napier, Director of the Primate Biology Program at the Smithsonian Institution.

4 / Dr. Vladimir Markotic, a physical anthropologist from the University of Calgary in Alberta, Canada.

5 / Dr. Allan Bryan, Professor of Anthropology at the University of Alberta in Edmonton, Canada.

6 / Tom Allen, member of the editorial staff of the National Geographic Society.

7 / Dr. Osman Hill, Director of Yerkes Regional Primate Research Center at Emory University.

It would be very interesting to know what Bigfoot thought about this impressive lineup of scientists. After having been around for centuries, he might now be able to learn whether or not he actually existed.

30

A lot of work had been done on the Patterson film since the afternoon when it was shot. The best frames had been rephotographed and enlarged. Technicians had even worked out a way in which the film could be shown at only one-third of its original speed. Any part of the sequence could be examined under high magnification. This didn't make the jerky, out-of-focus film a work of art, but it made things easier for the scientists.

This time, every inch of the film was studied carefully in a session that lasted more than four hours. Not one of the men present even hinted that it might have been a hoax. They all agreed that to fake something like that would require enormous funds and an enormous knowledge of physiology, anatomy, photography, and human psychology. Patterson possessed none of these and didn't claim to. Besides, he was far too intelligent to think he could set up a hoax good enough to fool the top experts in their field. Neither would he risk embarrassing his friend Sanderson.

Argosy's experts didn't dare say that they were believers or unbelievers. Being scientists, they couldn't make any conclusions without more evidence. Except for Sanderson, who had spent forty years gathering "Abominable Snowman" material, Dr. Osman Hill was about the only one who went out on a limb. He was convinced that the creature in the film was manlike rather than apelike.

Dr. Wraight pointed out that land bridges between Siberi and Alaska had existed several times in the past million years and that a migration of these creatures from Asia would have been possible. There have never been apes on the North American continent, so the good doctor must have been referring to a migration of man. The American Indians and Eskimos came over on the land bridge from Siberia, so why couldn't Bigfoot's ancestors have come over the same way? he asked, in effect.

This was a question that Ivan Sanderson had been asking himself for a long time. If Bigfoot wasn't an ape, who was he? Were his ancestors the gigantic eight-to twelve-foot giants science calls *Gigantopithecus* whose remains had been unearthed in China? Or had he descended from Java Man, now called *Homo erectus,* or from Neanderthal Man, who is known to scientists as *Homo neanderthalensis?*

Nobody knows, but most of us, I'm sure, would like to believe that Bigfoot descended from a race of gentle giants.

The scientists who studied the film were unable to come to any hard and fast conclusions. Most of them, however, agreed on certain points. Patterson's film was the real thing. If not, it was one of the most elaborate and cleverly done hoaxes ever perpetrated and would have required a pile of money and a wealth of ingenuity. It was generally agreed, too, that the creature in the movie was a hominid—or manlike creature—of some still undetermined origin. And that was the problem they all agreed should be solved.

The only way to solve it, of course, would be to send expeditions into the wilderness and keep them there until they either capture Bigfoot or prove that he doesn't exist. So far, this hasn't been done. The scientists aren't going to take Bigfoot seriously until somebody leads one into their laboratory by the hand.

The general public, we all know, is intensely interested in Bigfoot. The issue of *Argosy* in which stills from Patterson's movie and Sanderson's account of his experience appeared sold out completely in the first week, and people clamored for more. A flood of letters followed from readers who wanted more information.

Patterson, too, was up to his armpits in mail. He also received a visitor with a rather unusual request. The visitor was an editor of *National Wildlife.* The magazine's readers had been begging for the full story on Bigfoot, and the editor had flown out to the West Coast to interview Patterson.

He hadn't come alone, though. A polygraph, or lie detector, operator was with him. The cautious editor was making very certain that his readers would get the truth, the whole truth, and nothing but the truth. Instead of chucking the two men out into the snow, Patterson readily agreed to take a lie-detector test. The results convinced the experienced polygraph operator that his subject hadn't told any lies.

Not everyone, of course, believed Patterson. An obscure professor of zoology at an obscure college in California saw the film and reviewed it in the college paper. "I saw nothing in the film that would make me believe the creature exists," he wrote, "because everything I saw is within the possibility of a hoax. I place this idiocy in the same category as dragons, leprechauns, and the Great Pumpkin."

I'll bet people who believe in dragons and leprechauns, and especially the Great Pumpkin, are a lot more fun than that professor!

31

Stevenson, Washington, is a lovely little town that nestles on the north bank of the mighty Columbia River. It has one motel, one stop light, no parking meters, and no smog. It's the county seat of Skamania County and has 927 warm-hearted and friendly inhabitants.

There are only 5,230 people in all of Skamania County and most of them live close to the river.

Skamania County is mountainous, primitive, and savagely beautiful. Dense forests stretch from the Columbia to the slopes of Mount Adams and Mount Saint Helens. There are dozens of lakes and streams full of brook and rainbow trout, steelhead, salmon, and bass. Raccoons, porcupines, rabbits, deer, bears, coyotes, cougars, bobcats, and elk all live in the forests—and so does Bigfoot. Ape Canyon, where the giant hairy apes attacked the five miners in their cabin, is in Skamania County, and Jim Carter, the skier, disappeared in the same area. Roger Patterson searched for Bigfoot in Ape Canyon, and so have many others.

In the first few months of 1969 a whole rash of Bigfoot reports reached Stevenson. The winter was a particularly severe one and it was believed that heavy snows had forced the creatures out of the mountains in search of food. One family claimed that the "thing" lived close to their home all winter. They owned a large watchdog that almost went crazy with fright when the creature cut loose with one of its inhuman screams.

"I've never been so scared in my life," the woman of the house said. "I was just getting out of my car one night when the thing screamed. I jumped so hard that I banged my head on the ceiling of the car."

Two men who had shot a deer out of season were carrying it out of the mountains when they bumped into "a huge, apelike creature all covered with fur or hair." The men dropped the deer, turned tail, and got out of there fast. An hour or so later, they worked up enough nerve to go back. All they found was skin, crushed bones, and enormous footprints in the bloody snow. "That thing coulda tore an elephant apart," one declared.

A sighting early on the morning of March 5 sent dozens of people off into the forests and mountains in search of Bigfoot. Don Cox had just come around a corner east of Beacon Rock when he saw "a dark-colored creature with a face like an ape" crossing the road in front of him. In his report to the Skamania County sheriff's office, Cox said that "the beast was between 8 and 10 feet tall, ran like a man, and was covered with fuzzy fur."

Cox was going to the Columbia River to do some salmon fishing that morning. He had slowed down because of fog. As he got into the clear, he saw what he at first thought was a tree leaning toward the middle of the road. He slowed down even more and turned his headlights to high beam. It was then he saw what looked like a fur-covered human form with a face like an ape. The creature ran across the road in front of his car, leaped up a forty-degree bank, and disappeared into the woods.

"I was really shook and I stopped at a café in North Bonneville for a coffee," he said. "I told my story to a waitress and she called the sheriff's office."

Cox was still badly shaken by his experience, but he accompanied a deputy sheriff to the place where he had seen Bigfoot. They couldn't find any clear footprints, but they could see where a large creature of some type had gone up the bank. It had made an eight-foot jump and crushed a small fir tree when it landed.

Roy Craft, editor and publisher of *The Skamania County Pioneer*, interviewed Cox to assure himself that it was not a hoax. "I cannot vouch for what Cox saw. I can say I'm convinced he saw something out of the ordinary and has been honest in his effort to report it as he saw it in the glare of his headlights," he wrote.

A few days after Cox's sighting, a woman phoned Sheriff Bill Clossner and told him that there were some enormous footprints on her property. Clossner, Craft, and writer-photographer Ed McLarney rushed out and found that the woman hadn't exaggerated. The footprints were a whopping 22 inches long and 7½ inches wide. "Only a giant could have feet that size," mused the sheriff.

Bigfoot Research Association was told about the sightings in Skamania County, and members came over from Portland, Oregon, to investigate. They were well equipped. They brought not only horses with them but also a helicopter capable of carrying five men.

Luck was with them. They sighted Bigfoot twice from the air and twice from horseback. On one occasion they got within very close range. "The beast shrieked, growled, and let out a series of eerie, high-pitched shrieks that made our hair stand on end," one reported.

"After what I've seen in the last three weeks," another said, "I'm ready to believe just about anything."

Half of Skamania County, it seemed, was out looking for Bigfoot. "I was even awakened from a sound sleep by two nice little ladies who knocked on my door and asked where they could see the monster," a state park ranger at Beacon Rock told Roy Craft.

32

Because of the tremendous interest in Bigfoot, *The Skamania County Pioneer* came out with a Special Bigfoot Edition in the summer of 1969. The issue was sold out almost at once. I was able to get a couple of copies only through the kindness of Roy Craft, who had kept a few of them in his files.

"Readers are entitled to know whether or not the editor believes in Bigfoot," Mr. Craft wrote in his introduction to the Special Bigfoot Edition.

> To be honest, I think there is such a creature and I think that more than one was forced down out of the high mountain lava cave area by the most severe winter in the history of the Cascades.
>
> From the Ape Caves of Mt. St. Helens to the jungle-like lava bed country northeast of Carson, there is ample room for thousands of the creatures, although no one knows how many really exist.
>
> When Don Cox first reported seeing a Bigfoot on the Evergreen Highway near Beacon Rock, my first move was to check on the circumstances of his sighting and to assure myself it was not a hoax. As I remarked at that time in my editorial column, I satisfied myself that he was sincere.

Subsequent sightings were similarly checked out.

When footprints were being investigated by the County Sheriff's Office, I personally witnessed the professional manner in which the investigations were carried on.

Journalistically, the ape, or sub-human, is beyond the experience of *The Skamania County Pioneer*. But, evidence exists in sufficient quantity to make certain something is living on the fringes of humanity which bears scientific investigation.

The shadow world of the Gifford Pinchot National Forest of Skamania County holds many strange things not yet experienced by man, and each day something new is in store for the explorers of these wilds.

The friendly people of Skamania County are genuinely fond of Bigfoot and proud of the fact that he has chosen to live in their area. The following letter appeared in the Special Bigfoot Edition and is typical of the way most people in the county feel about their elusive Snowman:

Stevenson, Wash.

Dear Roy,

Upon reading your article about the Bigfoot in the March 14 *Pioneer*, I am of the opinion that this article is the best, and by far the most equitable, that I have seen.

In fairness to everyone and to all the stories concerning Bigfoot, Snowman, Yeti, etc., that have appeared throughout the years, my opinion is that you did a splendid job of "cutting it down the middle."

After studying reports of this creature's appearance in British Columbia, Oregon, California and here, my belief is that if this monster (and what right have we to call it that?) truly exists, it is unquestionably of high intelligence, intellect, culture and refinement; for these reasons:

1. It shuns civilization and seeks no association with mankind.

2. It has never robbed a garden, henhouse, broken a fence, injured a domestic animal or inconsiderately thrown bottles, cans and other litter along our beautiful streams, rivers, lakes and picnic grounds.

3. Despite its reported size and obvious power, it has never robbed an elderly lady of her purse, beaten up an aged and infirm man with a tire chain, molested a child or violated any of the rules of man or The Almighty.

There are many other reasons that could be expressed, all in favor of this splendid creature. It observes the Golden Rule as closely as do the rest of us.

Therefore, if it should be the good fortune of any of us to actually see this Bigfoot, let us consider ourselves to be fortunate. Do not attempt to harass it or molest it in any way, bearing in mind that it has not attempted to harm any of us or our possessions, nor has there been any evidence that it is creating smog or depleting our natural resources.

Should it appear in anyone's back yard and show signs of hunger, offer it a head of lettuce, a sandwich or anything else it might show interest in.

Unquestionably, it is self-supporting, owes no debts to anyone and asks for nothing but its God given right to live its own life with malice toward none.

However, it may someday seek to make friends with the right people and, if we treat it decently, we shall learn more about it than all the pursuits and costly research activities could ever produce.

We have much to be thankful for in this magnificent area. Let us all try to recognize this fact and appreciate and cherish the beautiful, natural environment surrounding us. If it exists, the Bigfoot can be rightfully accepted as an attribute, a citizen of good standing and a welcome addition to Skamania County.

This is a warm-hearted, broadminded community, but to those on the outside who might come here merely out of curiosity, litter our roads and byways with bottles, tin cans, cigarette packages and other trash; break down fences, trample gardens and "horrify the livestock," my advice is: "Find a Bigfoot in your own area and keep your business at home."

Yours,
J.A. Minsy.

Roy Craft, Don Cox, members of Bigfoot Research Association, and many others are convinced that Bigfoot is roaming happily around in the remote wilderness areas of Skamania County. A few are more cautious. When asked if he believed in the existence of Bigfoot, Sheriff Bill Clossner replied, "Well, I lean awfully hard in that direction."

Writer, photographer, and enthusiastic outdoorsman Ed McLarney says, "By training, I was doubtful, but after seeing the tracks and hearing the stories from people who have seen Bigfoot, I'm now 90 percent sure that something exists which is beyond my own experience."

Although the people in Stevenson and the surrounding area are pleased that Bigfoot is a citizen of their county, they can still enjoy a laugh at his expense. One example is the following letter, which appeared in the Special Bigfoot Edition. It was written soon after Don Cox had sighted the creature early on a foggy morning.

Stevenson, Wash.

Dear Mr. Craft,

I thoroughly enjoyed your recent *Pioneer* story of the Snowman. Much as I like detracting from what anyone reports, I must say that from the description presented, it was no Snowman, but merely my mother-in-law that was seen.

She is addicted to early morning walks, and being nosey likes to see what people do before the average person arises. She does have a frightful appearance, but is not as tall as reported.

No doubt distortion caused by the early morning fog is responsible for the seemingly unusual height.

As for leaping up the bank, it may well be that Mr. Cox, coming out of the fog, may have been driving close to the shoulder of the road as is common with careful drivers, and mother, thinking she might be struck, dashed madly for safety. (A bit foggy herself, both she and the motorist could have been understandably confused.)

To all who may see this alleged Snowman, I beseech you not to shoot at it or otherwise attempt to harm it, because it is probably my mother-in-law. Although harmless, do not invite her into your home as she will immediately become domineering, critical and make loud, unpleasant noises.

Like any other red-blooded, two-fisted, boss-of-the-house husband, I must request you to please withhold my name if you print this. My wife and mother-in-law would clobber me and I'd lose what few fishing rights I now have.

Sincerely,
Al Baker.

Alarmed by the growing number of hunters who were roaming through the mountains hoping to get a shot at Bigfoot, Roy Craft met with the Board of County Commissioners of Skamania County. As a result of the meeting, Ordinance No. 69–01 was drawn and passed. The ordinance imposed a $10,000 fine and up to five years' imprisonment for shooting Bigfoot.

"Although the ordinance was adopted April 1, this is not an April Fool's Day joke," said Board Chairman Conrad Lundy, Jr. "There is reason to believe such an animal exists, and there is even more reason to make its slaying unlawful in order to prevent accidents caused by the use of lethal weapons in the search."

Now that Bigfoot was protected by Ordinance No. 69–01, he probably slept much better at night.

33

By 1972 little Stevenson had become the nerve center for Bigfoot expeditions. More reports of sightings came from Washington than from either California, Oregon, or British Columbia.

The fact that far more sightings were reported by individuals than expeditions isn't really surprising. People in the West love the out-of-doors and there are always hunters, fishermen, skiers, and hikers in the wilderness area, as well as loggers and timber surveyors. A number of sightings were also reported by people who had seen Bigfoot while driving along lonely roads. Don Cox, of course, sighted the creature on a well-traveled highway.

Mrs. Louis Baxter has the unusual distinction of having seen Bigfoot on two different occasions. The first time, she was coming home around ten o'clock at night and a huge dark-gray, shaggy-haired "something" crossed the road in front of her. For one horrible second, she thought that she was going to hit it. She swerved sharply, however, and the "something" made it safely across the road. Mrs. Baxter didn't get a good look at it, but she saw that the creature was running on two legs and was huge and hairy.

She saw the "something" again in 1972 and got a much closer look than she really wanted. She was driving in the same general area where Don Cox had seen Bigfoot three years earlier. Her car was making an odd sound and she stopped to investigate. The tires were all right, so she bent down to see if there might be something stuck under the fenders that was making the noise.

Suddenly Mrs. Baxter had the prickly feeling that she was being watched. Without straightening up, she looked toward the wooded area beside the road, "and I found myself looking straight into the face of the biggest creature I have ever seen. It was ten or twelve feet tall and terribly ugly."

The Bigfoot seen by Mrs. Baxter was a sort of coconut brown, shaggy and dirty-looking. Although it was holding one huge fist up to its mouth and might have been eating something, she could see a row of large, square, white teeth. The head was big and seemed to be set right onto a pair of powerful shoulders. The hair on the head was about two inches long and may have covered the ears, because she couldn't see them.

The jaw jutted out past the nose, which had wide, flaring nostrils. The nose and upper lip appeared to be less hairy than the rest of the face. It had a small forehead that slanted backward. Mrs. Baxter thought that the eyes in particular were most unusual. They were amber-colored and seemed to glow like an animal's eyes at night when the lights of a car shine on them.

Mrs. Baxter readily admits that Bigfoot gave her the fright of her life. "I've never been so terrified," she says. "I screamed or hollered, but I was so scared that I don't know whether any sound came out or not. Anyway, the creature never moved. It just stood there looking at me with its huge fist up by the mouth. I can't remember how I got back into the car or how I started it."

None of the expeditions had Mrs. Baxter's kind of luck. One group with the horrible name of American Yeti Expedition did, however, have some exciting moments. Robert W. Morgan of Miami, Florida, had invented a sound device with which he hoped to attract Bigfoot. The group found some fairly fresh tracks measuring sixteen inches long one day, and Morgan decided to try his invention at that spot.

And it seems to have worked! Some brand-new tracks were found in the area next morning, but Bigfoot—or Yeti—had already taken off for parts unknown and no one caught so much as a glimpse of him. It was a highly encouraging sign. It was the only time, though, that Bigfoot came around to see what all the noise was about. Having satisfied his curiosity, he probably felt that there was no sense in going back for another look.

Morgan has already led two expeditions into the Mount Saint Helens wilderness and is planning more. He still has faith in his sound device, but all he'll say about it is that it has a high-pitched bell tone. He's afraid that someone may make something similar and attract Bigfoot to a home or campsite where he might do some damage.

The third American Yeti Expedition will be more sophisticated than the first two. There will be more searchers and more equipment. Morgan hopes to attract Bigfoot to drugged bait, then shoot him with a drug-filled dart.

He knows, of course, that if anything goes wrong, he'll be in big trouble for breaking Skamania County's Ordinance No. 69–01. It could mean a $10,000 fine and five years in the Stevenson jailhouse.

This would probably please Sheriff Bill Clossner, though. There's hardly ever anyone in the Stevenson jail and he sometimes gets rather lonely.

34

Ron Olson is a pleasant, ruggedly handsome man in his early thirties. He lives in Eugene, Oregon, and is the executive director of North American Wildlife Research Association. The goal of his organization is to capture Bigfoot alive and bring him in for scientific study.

A few years ago Olson gave up a profitable film-distributing business to devote all of his time and energy to Bigfoot. He works closely with John Green and several other researchers and they share much of their information. By feeding this information into a computer, they have learned a great deal about the creature and his habits. They have also learned that there's still a great deal more to be learned.

The greatest number of reported sightings have been in Humboldt County, California, in Skamania County, Washington, and in the area around Harrison Hot Springs, British Columbia, which is where John Green lives. That doesn't necessarily mean, though, that there are more Bigfoot there than in other places. Far more people are searching in these areas, so it's natural that more sightings would be reported. On one occasion, there were eight expeditions in the Bluff Creek area at the same time. The fact that Bigfoot has been sighted far oftener during the day than at night really proves nothing, either. For one thing, a man has a hard time seeing in the dark. Besides, very few people are poking around in the forests and mountains in the dead of night. Both Ron Olson and John Green believe that the creature is nocturnal and only goes out during the day when he feels like it or when he can't get to sleep.

If you live in an area where signs of Bigfoot have been reported, here's what you do if you want to see him: get on your bicycle at night and ride along the lonely wilderness roads. This might mean a million or so miles of pedaling before you see one, but that can't be helped. Bigfoot has been sighted on roads more often than any other place and most of those times he was seen at night. July, August, and September are the best months to look for him.

Ron Olson's North American Wildlife Research Association covers a lot of ground. Whenever a sighting is reported, men go out to investigate. Expeditions are sent into regions where there have been a number of reports, and they stay there for as long as possible. They're equipped with tranquilizing guns and 16 mm. movie equipment. Like the American Yeti Expedition, they also use sound devices, which they hope will attract the creature to them.

Very little information sneaks past Olson. People living in places from which Bigfoot reports have come are requested to keep him informed of any new developments. Sheriffs' offices, forest ranger stations, and newspapers throughout the Pacific Northwest are in constant contact with him. If Bigfoot is seen anywhere in the huge primitive area that stretches from California to British Columbia, chances are high that Olson will hear about it. He already has reports of several hundred sightings in his card files.

Ron's pet project is a huge cage that he designed and had built. Knowing that Bigfoot is a curious fellow and will eat almost anything, he has baited the trap with an assortment of goodies. If hunger or curiosity leads the creature into the trap, an electronically controlled door will slam down and Bigfoot will be out of circulation for a while. "I know that the trap works," Ron chuckles, "because I've already caught two bears and an Indian."

It is my personal opinion that of all the individuals and organizations who are after Bigfoot, Ron Olson's North American Wildlife Research Association has the best chance of capturing him. Ron has dedicated his life to this purpose. There is no doubt at all in his mind that the creature exists. Although they've never met officially, Ron is genuinely fond of Bigfoot and his enthusiasm infects everyone he talks to. Ron himself is confident of success, and those who know him wish him the best of luck.

John Green, on the other hand, is interested in Bigfoot from a purely scientific point of view. He wants one to be brought in either dead or alive and he really doesn't care who does it. His wish is to prove to the scientific world that there actually are such creatures. It bothers him not at all that someone else will have to furnish the proof. "I have few qualifications as a hunter," he says, "and no expectation of being the man who comes home with a sasquatch."

Why, you might ask, are all these expeditions and individuals so determined to capture poor old Bigfoot?

Well, there are a number of reasons. Roger Patterson told Jim McClarin that he had three reasons for wanting to capture the creature: first, to prove to the world that this humanoid creature exists; second, for the personal fame that he would receive; and third, for the money he would get for his accounts and movies of the capture.

The thoughts of fame and fortune have undoubtedly driven many men into the wilderness. "If I capture Bigfoot," one declared flatly, "I'll be a world-famous multimillionaire." The late Tom Slick, of course, had been a well-known multimillionaire long before he organized the Pacific Northwest Expedition, which spent three years searching in primitive areas. He had need for neither fame nor fortune, so his interest was probably one of intellectual curiosity.

It's most likely the thrill of the chase that sends the great majority of people off in search of Bigfoot. They're looking for excitement, and few things could be more exciting than bumping into a hairy, eight-foot-tall monster in the depths of a dark forest. It might, in fact, be far more exciting than the searcher had bargained for. A number of tough outdoorsmen have confessed that they fled at the sight of Bigfoot; others found the experience so terrifying that their minds refused to accept what they had seen.

35

Shortly before midnight on June 25, 1973, a young couple sat talking in a parked car on the Murphysboro boat ramp. The silence of the starry night was suddenly shattered by an unearthly scream that very nearly sent them through the roof of the car. "What in the world was that?" the girl cried out in alarm.

Before her companion had a chance to tell her that he couldn't imagine what it was, they both saw an enormous hairy creature about eight feet tall walking toward them. The monster was light-colored, but it must have been wallowing around on the bank of the river because it was all matted with mud. The couple stared, not really believing what they were seeing. When the monster kept coming, however, the man started his car and beat it out of there. He drove straight to the police station and filed an "unknown creature" report.

The police took the matter seriously. They knew the young couple well and it was obvious that they had had a severe fright. The police also knew that the two people wouldn't want anyone to know that they had been together. The fact that they were seeing one another was supposed to be a secret. Now there was a good chance that their names would be in the newspapers. "They wouldn't have risked all that if they weren't really scared," said one of the policemen.

Officer Jimmie Nash later went down to the river to have a look around. When he returned, he was a firm believer. "I was leaning over inspecting some tracks in the mud, when something let out the most incredible shriek I've ever heard," he told his fellow officers. "It came from the bushes near the bank. I knew that it wasn't a bobcat or screech owl, so I high-tailed it back to the car."

The local newspaper gave the incident only a couple of short paragraphs on the third page the following day. Much to the relief of the embarrassed couple who had filed an "unknown creature" report, their names weren't mentioned.

But there was going to be a lot more excitement in Murphysboro in the weeks ahead. The afternoon after the first sighting was reported, four-year-old Christian Baril was in his backyard chasing butterflies with a glass jar. Suddenly he dropped his jar and raced into the house. "Daddy, Daddy," he called. "There's a great big ghost out in back!"

Mr. Baril went outdoors to take a look and saw a huge, hairy monster disappearing into the bush. He thought his eyes were playing tricks on him, so he said nothing until the following day, when the Murphysboro Monster made big news.

Randy Creath and Cheryl Ray were talking on Cheryl's front porch that night when something moved in the brush nearby. Cheryl went to turn on a light and Randy went to investigate.

At that moment, the thing that had been making the noise stepped out of the bushes.

Towering over the terror-stricken teen-aged couple was a creature resembling an enormous gorilla. It was at least eight feet tall. It was covered with shaggy, matted, dirty-white hair and had a foul smell like river slime. The two teen-agers shook with fright as they stared at the ugly beast. The beast also stared at them from a distance of only fifteen feet away. After what seemed like a lifetime—but was perhaps no more than thirty long seconds—the creature turned around and crashed off through the brush in the direction of the river.

Cheryl and Randy rushed straight to the police station and reported their terrifying experience. Randy was the son of a state trooper and he drew a picture of the creature for the police officers.

Their story convinced the police that they had seen something entirely out of the ordinary—a something that could endanger the lives of innocent people. Police Chief Toby Berger immediately ordered his entire force out for an all-night search. Jerry Nellis brought Reb along to help with the tracking. Reb was a large German shepherd that could track just about anything.

Officers with floodlights soon discovered a rough trail in the brush. Grass was crushed and broken branches dangled. Small trees had been snapped off just above ground level. Reb stayed on the scent and led Nellis and Nash to an abandoned barn on the old Buller farm.

That was as far as Reb wanted to go. He went up to the door, yelped, then backed off in panic. Nellis picked the dog up and threw it through the doorway. Reb wanted none of it. He came straight back out, his hackles standing on end, and whining like a puppy. Officer Nash radioed for help and fourteen police cars rushed to the scene. The barn was searched thoroughly, but there was no sign of the creature.

"A lot of things in life can't be explained," said Police Chief Berger, "and this is one of them. We don't know what the creature is, but we do believe that what these people saw was real. We've tracked it and the dog got a definite scent. And whatever it smelled scared poor Reb half to death."

Chief Berger couldn't have known it at the time, but he was going to hear a lot more about the Murphysboro Monster.

36

All was quiet for a time, then Mrs. Nedra Green phoned the police one night. "There's something out by my shed," she said in a frightened voice, "and every once in a while it lets out with a shrill, piercing scream. I don't know what it is, but I'm all alone out here and I'm afraid. Is there anything that you can do?"

The police rushed out to the isolated farmhouse at once. Reb, the tracking dog, was with them and he picked up the scent immediately. It went in the direction of the river, but Reb had had enough. Nothing his owner did or said could persuade the dog to go any farther. He wasn't on the police payroll and he saw no reason to risk his life and not get a single penny for it.

After assuring Mrs. Green that there was nothing to be afraid of, the officers drove down to the river.

From time to time they heard strange splashing noises that sounded like something floundering through knee-deep water. They searched the riverbank for hours, but finally had to give up.

Later in the summer of 1973 the Miller Carnival was set up in Riverside Park, not far from the boat ramp. This was a big event for all the youngsters and for quite a few adults as well. They rode on the Ferris wheel, threw balls at bottles, ate too many hot dogs, drank root beer, and did all the other fun things that people do at carnivals.

The Miller Carnival had enjoyed three successful days when an uninvited visitor presented himself. He arrived at two o'clock in the morning and he hadn't paid to get in. That visitor was what the people called the Murphysboro Monster. Once again, Bigfoot's curiosity had gotten the best of him.

The day's festivities were over and only carnival workers were still on the grounds at that hour. Three of them—Otis Norris, Ray Adkerson and Wesley Lavander—were going about their business when they noticed that the ponies were acting very strangely indeed. Normally the ponies were gentle creatures that walked around in circles with small children on their backs. After finishing their work, the littke fellows were tied to some bushes for the night.

The three men couldn't imagine what was going on. The ponies shied, rolled their eyes, and tried desperately to pull themselves free. "Let's have a look," Norris said. "There's something wrong here."

They hurried over, and there, standing upright in the darkness, was a creature weighing about four hundred pounds. It was eight feet tall, light-colored, and completely covered with hair. It didn't act menacing but only seemed to be interested in the ponies.

The creature disappeared before anyone else arrived. An hour later, however, it was back. Carnival worker Charles Kimbal went to check on the ponies when they again tried to pull free, and there was Bigfoot. The ponies apparently intrigued him and he had come back for another look.

The carnival operators decided not to report the matter to the police until the carnival was ready to leave Murphysboro. They were afraid that business would suffer if people knew that the monster was in the area.

"This is no hoax," said Tony Stevens, the Murphysboro newspaper editor, when the "unknown creature" report was finally filed. "This is hunting country, you know, and anyone silly enough to go around in an animal costume is going to get his butt shot off."

As soon as the report got out, hundreds of men and boys armed with rifles and shotguns rushed out to Riverside Park. Curious women and children also thronged through the wooded region. Afraid that someone would be killed. Police Chief Berger ordered the park to be closed to anyone carrying a weapon.

Sightings continued to be reported throughout the rest of the summer and early fall. People slept with loaded rifles beside their beds and many children stayed home on Halloween. They were too afraid of the Murphysboro Monster to do any trick-or-treating in 1973.

The police were completely baffled and not really sure what to do. It was finally decided to ask Harlan Sorkin, an expert on such creatures, to come to Murphysboro and try to solve the mystery.

Sorkin investigated the matter thoroughly. He then told the police that the descriptions matched those of hundreds of similar sightings that had been reported in North America in the last decade. "The creatures are called Bigfoot," he said. "They're generally shy and placid, but they have the strength of five men and there are stories saying that they have attacked and killed people."

The people now know that the Murphysboro Monster is a Bigfoot, but it's not known whether that knowledge provides much consolation.

The full account of the Murphysboro Monster appeared in the November 1, 1973, edition of *The New York Times.*

The most incredible part about this incredible story is that Murphysboro is approximately 1,500 miles from the Pacific Northwest, which is Bigfoot Country. Murphysboro is on the bank of the Mississippi River in southern Illinois!

So what was Bigfoot doing so far from home? And how did he get there? He doesn't own a car and he doesn't have any money for plane, train, or bus tickets. And even with his four- to five-foot strides, he'd hardly be interested in walking 1,500 miles.

Nobody seems to know how he got there. The good people of Murphysboro, Illinois, might sleep better, though, if they knew that reports of other Bigfoot sightings have come in from almost every state in the American Middle West and so far he hasn't bothered a single soul in that whole vast area. He's scared a few people out of their wits, it's true, but it's not Bigfoot's fault that he's so big and ugly.

37

In his latest book, *The Sasquatch File,* John Green reports that Bigfoot has been sighted in Illinois on *eight* different occasions, and this doesn't include the recent visit by the Murphysboro Monster. This means that only California, Oregon, and Washington have more Bigfoot sightings on record than the far-away prairie state of Illinois.

Bigfoot, or a close relative of his, has also allegedly been seen in Pennsylvania, North Carolina, Georgia, Florida, Arkansas, Ohio, Indiana, Michigan, Minnesota, Wisconsin, Iowa, Missouri, Nebraska, Idaho, Alaska, and, of course, Texas.

Green readily admits that many of the reports he receives from states east of the Pacific mountain ranges come from sources that are not too convincing. Quite a few of them, in fact, are from people who claim that they saw a giant, hairy creature one night while they were out looking for flying saucers. Many also come from people who fail to give any details. They simply write to him and say that they saw a huge beast that looked like an ape and let it go at that.

Mr. Green is a full-time sasquatch researcher and an extremely thorough one. He can't very well go dashing off from British Columbia to Florida or some other faroff place, though, if someone writes to him and claims that he's seen a big apelike thing behind his chicken coop. There have been so many Bigfoot sightings in the Pacific Northwest in recent years that he can't possibly keep up with all of them, much less fly all the way across the continent to check on something that might amount to nothing.

Some of the "monster" stories that have come out of the Middle Western states, however, are highly convincing and most likely true. One of them, in fact, appeared in the June, 1966, issue of *True* magazine. The article was entitled "The Hellzapoppin' Hunt for the Michigan Monster."

All the action started in the summer of 1964 near Sister lakes. Reports kept coming into the police station from people who claimed that they'd seen a nine-foot monster that must have weighed over five hundred pounds. "It cries like a baby and makes the earth tremble when it walks," one man told the police. "It looks like an ape and its eyes shine in the dark."

The police were naturally somewhat skeptical at first. A monster had absolutely no business being in Michigan and they knew it. But more and more people insisted that they had seen a monster, and in a few cases their hair was still standing on end when they made their report. Police officials investigated and found giant, humanlike footprints that no human could have made. They were seventeen inches long, six inches wide across the ball of the foot, and four inches across the heel. The policemen looked at one another and shook their heads. There certainly seemed to be a monster in the area all right, but what could they do about it? they wondered. Monsters weren't even mentioned in any of the police manuals. Besides, the creature hadn't committed any crime, so they couldn't put out a warrant for its arrest.

Reports continued to trickle in from time to time. All the sightings except one took place at night. In that case the creature scared the daylights out of two young girls who met it on a wooded road one sunny afternoon. "Except for the face, it was just like a bear walking on its hind legs," they told the police in quaking voices.

Men found the tracks, but nothing else. The monster had disappeared and no more was heard about it for several months. Suddenly, however, it popped up again near the little town of Munroe, not far from Sister Lakes. And this time, Bigfoot very nearly got himself into serious trouble!

Seventeen-year-old Christine Van Acker and her mother, Mrs. George Owens, were on their way home one hot night in August. Christine was driving through a stretch of forest only a few hundred yards from their farmhouse when a gigantic hairy form loomed up right in front of them. "Don't stop, Christine!" yelled her mother. "Don't stop!"

Christine was too terrified to know what she was doing. In her horror, she slammed on the brakes, skidded into the monster, and killed the engine on her car. The creature reached through the window, put a huge hairy hand on top of Christine's head, and slammed her face against the doorpost.

Both women were shrieking and the horn was blaring so loudly that people at the farmhouse came rushing out to see what was happening. They found Mrs. Owens hysterical and Christine unconscious. The creature had gone back into the forest. The unfortunate incident reached the police and the press and the hunt for the Michigan Monster was on in a big way.

Armed men and tracking dogs combed the woods and fields for days on end. The creature had finally misbehaved and they were determined to hunt it down and destroy it. The trouble was, though, that there was absolutely no sign of the creature to be found. It had simply disappeared, and the mystery of the Michigan Monster is still a mystery.

38

Wisconsin shares a border with both Michigan and Illinois. It's only fair, therefore, that Wisconsin should also have a monster. The creature was sighted in the Deltox Marsh near Fremont in the fall of 1968, and Ivan Sanderson hurried out from New York to investigate. Mr. Sanderson was then the director of the Society for the Investigation of the Unexplained. His article, "Wisconsin's Abominable Snowman," appeared in *Argosy* magazine in April, 1969.

Unlike the Murphysboro Monster and the Michigan Monster, Wisconsin's Abominable Snowman didn't really frighten anyone. It's probably true, too, that the monsters in Murphysboro and Munroe didn't frighten anyone on purpose. They seem to be extremely curious creatures who like to know what's going on. There's even the possibility that the Michigan Monster put his hand on Christine Van Acker's head because he wanted to be friendly.

Or maybe that was Bigfoot's way of showing Christine that he wasn't angry because her car had skidded into him. It's not known whether the creature actually slammed her head against the doorpost or whether Christine jerked her head away in stark terror and slammed it against the doorpost herself.

Wisconsin's Abominable Snowman was first seen by Bob Parry, Dick Bleier, and Bill Mallo while bow-and-arrow hunting in the Deltox Marsh. They came into a clearing and there stood what looked like a large and powerfully built man covered with short, very dark hair. As soon as the creature saw the men, it moved swiftly off into the brush. All the men agreed that neither a bear nor a man could move with such speed.

On the last day of November, the same three men were back in the marsh with nine other hunters on a deer drive. Instead of flushing a deer, however, they flushed an Abominable Snowman. This time the creature didn't dash off into the brush. It moved away leisurely and seemingly unafraid. Every once in a while, it would glance over is shoulder and look back at the hunters. It was obviously curious and didn't act at all menacing. The creature walked like a man and swung its long arms back and forth. The twelve men all agreed that the manlike creature they saw was approximately eight feet tall, extremely heavy, and completely covered with dark hair.

Four more men later reported that they had also seen the creature, and word reached Ivan Sanderson in New York. He hurried out and soon found fresh tracks in the snow. After measuring them, photographing them, and studying them at great length, he came to the conclusion that the giant footprints were identical to those he had seen in the Pacific Northwest.

The giant monster that had been sighted in the Deltox Marsh, he told the citizens of Fremont, was an
Abominable Snowman—a manlike creature that was
known as Bigfoot in California, Oregon, and Washington and known to Canadians as sasquatch.

Not wishing to be left out of things, Missouri came
up with a monster of its own in 1972. *The New York
Times* printed the story of the Missouri Monster on
July 30 and other papers from coast to coast gave detailed accounts. Monsters always fire people's imagi-
nations, and the one in Missouri was no exception.

Some solid and sincere citizens filed convincing reports, which were thoroughly investigated by the police and press. One terror-stricken young woman
claimed that a strange creature grabbed her four-year-
old nephew in the backyard of her home and started
running off with him. It dropped the child, though,
when the woman screamed and the dog chased it. "I
thought it was a bear," she told the police, "but I
showed my nephew a picture of a gorilla and he said
the thing looked like that."

In another report, a boy of eight was playing in the
yard when he saw "a big hairy thing with a dog under
its arm." He ran into the house and told his fifteen-
year-old sister about it. She looked out the window
and saw the creature standing in a ditch. It was at least
seven feet tall and ran off on two legs.

As always happens in these cases, a number of reports came in that were simply ignored. They came
from people who were either crackpots or publicity-
mad. One insisted that the creature he had seen was
half-horse and half-man. Another claimed that a huge
hairy monster about ten feet high had leaped out of a

tree and chased him for nearly a mile. It's unfortunate that people report happenings that are obviously untrue, but there are certain individuals who will say almost anything to get their names in the paper.

The Missouri Monster disappeared as suddenly as it had appeared, and now Hollywood decided to cash in on the Midwest Monster Mystery. To the relief of serious Bigfoot researchers and those who had sighted the creature or seen its tracks, the film was totally unlike *King Kong* or *The Planet of the Apes*.

The Legend of Foggy Bottom was an authentic and serious movie that held the interest of everyone who saw it. There was no Hollywood sensationalism involved. It was a factual account of a small community in Arkansas that had been terrorized for years by some giant, hairy, manlike creature. The producer had the good sense not to have the special-effects people create a man-made monster to add extra thrills, and not a single monster appears anywhere in the film.

There were no Hollywood actors in the cast. The heroes were simple, honest, hardworking people who lived in and around the Arkansas community. Many of them had seen something that they couldn't understand. An enormous creature of some kind was haunting the area. It had been seen by men, women, and children, and they were terrified. The once peaceful little community now lived in constant fear.

The Legend of Foggy Bottom is the story told by these people. They're not crackpots and they're not publicity-seekers. They simply told what they had seen and they told the truth. Truth is often stranger than fiction, and this was proved in a sincere and honest way in *The Legend of Foggy Bottom*.

People who saw the film were greatly impressed.

Perhaps they didn't believe in dragons, leprechauns, or the Great Pumpkin, but many of them were now ready to believe that there actually are monsters in the United States.

39

The fact that Bigfoot has been seen in the American Middle West isn't really as surprising as it may seem. A land bridge between Asia and North America has existed several times in the past million years. The Indians came over that way and so, apparently, did Bigfoot. It may have taken his family many thousands of years to get from Siberia to places like Illinois and Wisconsin, but he seems to have made it all right. If the Indians got that far, there's no reason why Bigfoot should have stayed behind.

Then why have people only seen him in recent years, you might ask. This isn't quite true. The New York *Evening Post* published a report of a great hairy giant as early as 1831, nearly 150 years ago. And the monster was sighted in—of all places—Missouri! *The New Orleans Times Picayune* carried a story in 1851 telling about "a giant wild man all covered with hair" that had been seen in—Arkansas! Several newspapers on the West Coast printed reports of hairy monsters and giant hairy apes during the 1850s, and there may have been earlier reports in many newspapers that no longer exist.

Bigfoot is a shy and elusive fellow who keeps pretty much to himself. His greatest downfall seems to be his curiosity. Every once in a while—as in the case of the Murphysboro Monster—he simply has to see what's going on. When he blunders into an inhabited area, there's always a fair chance that he'll be seen. If he's human, his intelligence would tell him to stay hidden. If he's not human, then his animal instincts would tell him to stay away from inhabited areas. Remember, too, that he's a nocturnal creature who makes his home in forested areas where few people venture after dark. Cougars are fairly common in many places in the Pacific Northwest, yet there are thousands of people who have spent much of their life in these forests and never seen one.

There are only a very few cases on record where people have gone out looking for Bigfoot and actually seen him. Ron Olson, John Green, Jim McClarin, and dozens of others have devoted years to the search and never laid eyes on one. Bigfoot has the habit of popping up out of nowhere, frightening some innocent soul half to death, and then vanishing into the wilderness. Many times, hundreds of men armed to the teeth go charging into the wilderness after him and the result is always the same. They see neither hide nor hair of the big fellow!

40

One of the many things that puzzles the Bigfoot researchers is the fact that males are sighted twenty times oftener than females or children. It's true that those who catch only fleeting glimpses of the creature aren't going to be certain of the sex. Neither are those who bump into one on a dark night. Christine Van Acker, for example, couldn't possibly have known whether it was a male or female Bigfoot that put a huge hairy hand on the top of her head.

Of the last 125 sightings reported to John Green, only 6 were said to be females, and 5 of these had a baby with them. Sightings of a Bigfoot family group are very rare indeed, although Albert Ostman claims to have spent six days with a family of four after being kidnapped by the father.

Whether Bigfoot is a good husband and daddy isn't known. It's possible, of course, that males have been seen so much oftener than females because they were out on a food-gathering mission when they were sighted. That may also account for the fact that they have frequently visited farmhouses. Mama and Baby Bigfoot were probably at home and Papa was out scrounging around for something to take back for dinner. Nearly everything, however, points to the fact that the family splits up once Baby Bigfoot is able to look after himself.

Newspapers constantly referred to *the* Murphysboro Monster, *the* Michigan Monster, and *the* Missouri Monster. The word *the* is sadly misleading in this case. It implies that one lone, mateless, childless, and parentless monster is poking around all by his lonely self in the Shawnee Forest, the woods of Michigan, and the forested hills of Missouri.

Only one monster may have been seen, yes, but it takes monsters to make monsters. The creatures that were seen almost certainly had friends or relatives hiding around somewhere in the area. Perhaps they don't see much of one another, but it's pretty hard to believe that there would be only one Bigfoot in Illinois, one more in Michigan, and another in Missouri. It's also pretty hard to believe that the monsters would make their way from Michigan to Wisconsin to Missouri to Illinois. Everything is still pretty much guesswork. If a monster has actually been seen in these places, though, then it's safe to assume that there are several more of them not too far away.

So why hasn't anyone ever found a dead Bigfoot or at least the skeleton of one, you might ask. All right. Ask anyone who spends a lot of time hunting whether he's ever found the skeleton of a bear, deer, rabbit, raccoon, squirrel, or any other animal lying around and he'll tell you that he hasn't. Nature just doesn't permit organic matter to lie about on the floor of the forest for very long. Rodents nibble on the bones, the sun bakes them, the cold freezes them, and the snow hides them. In a few seasons, they decompose into something completely unrecognizable. It's even possible that these creatures may dig a hole and bury their dead. Now that might sound pretty farfetched, but it might also be true.

Being such a big fellow, Bigfoot must spend most of his time trying to find something to eat. Fortunately he seems to be able to eat just about anything. Albert Ostman saw them eating nuts, spruce and hemlock twigs, and some kind of grass with long sweet roots. Bigfoot also digs for clams and crayfish and even goes into the creeks and rivers during the salmon runs. Indians dry their salmon, and there are many reports of Bigfoot taking salmon that had been hung up in the sun to dry. In one case he entered a shed in broad daylight and helped himself to a barrel of dried fish. After eating his fill, he amused himself by carrying the barrel outside and dumping the remainder all over the place.

Ten reports came in during a heavy salmon run on the Nooksack River near Marietta, Washington, in a period of just one week. Everyone, including Bigfoot, was there for the fish and the fun.

One man was drifting a gillnet behind his boat at night when he realized that something had gone wrong. Turning on his spotlight, he saw that an enormous hairy creature nearly nine feet tall was pulling on the far end of the net, evidently trying to get the fish that had been trapped in it. The man shouted at the top of his voice and two other men rushed to the scene and shone their lights on the creature. Bigfoot reluctantly let go of the net, waded ashore, and stalked off into the forest.

William Roe watched one of the giant creatures stripping leaves off bushes with its teeth. The creature has occasionally been seen in orchards, and a Washington man had to be taken to the hospital and treated for shock after bumping into one while checking his apples. There are many reports from people who have seen Bigfoot eating berries. The most dramatic one, however, comes from John Bringsli of Nelson, British Columbia.

Mr. Bringsli was out in the woods picking huckleberries when he glanced up and saw a great beast staring at him. It was standing about fifty feet away on a slight rise in the ground. The creature was seven to nine feet tall and the huge body was entirely covered with shaggy hair. It had very wide shoulders, a flat face, and long arms. Its apelike head appeared to be fastened directly to its shoulders.

For two full minutes, Bringsli and Bigfoot stood staring at one another. The man was paralyzed with fear. It wasn't until the giant creature began moving slowly toward him that John Bringsli was able to take action. Hurling his huckleberry bucket into the bushes, he whirled around and raced for his car. He was still shaking badly when he told his story to the Nelson *News*.

Bigfoot also eats meat when he can get it. Gary Joanis and Jim Newall of Oregon watched him pick up a deer they had shot, put it under his arm, and walk quickly back into the forest. Two Washington hunters who met Bigfoot dropped a deer they had been carrying and fled for their lives. When they returned to the spot some time later, they found only hair, crushed bones, and some enormous footprints in the bloody snow. There is evidence, too, that Bigfoot is quite capable of keeping himself well supplied with meat. He's been seen chasing cattle and he's been accused of stealing sheep, goats, and dogs.

And who knows? It may have been hunger rather than curiosity that prompted Bigfoot to pay two visits to the ponies at the Miller Carnival in Murphysboro's

Riverside Park. He certainly wasn't interested in going ponyback riding, so he may have been planning to take one home for dinner.

If he had a wife or girl friend hiding out somewhere in the nearby forest, the two of them could have enjoyed a lovely meal of raw pony.

41

Thanks largely to the efforts of men like John Green, Ron Olson, Jim McClarin, and a dozen or so others, scientists in the United States and Canada are at long last beginning to take Bigfoot seriously. Unlike the Abominable Snowmen, the evidence for the existence of Bigfoot is simply too overwhelming to ignore. Green alone has over eight hundred reports from people who have seen tracks or the creature itself.

Dr. John Napier, formerly Director of the Primate Biology Program at the Smithsonian Institution in Washington, D.C., is a very hard man to convince. In his book *Bigfoot: The Yeti and Sasquatch in Myth and Reality,* he discusses the Abominable Snowmen of Asia and Bigfoot of North America. If it were not for the footprint photographed by Eric Shipton, he says, he would simply dismiss the Abominable Snowmen as imaginary creatures that couldn't exist in the barren glaciers and snowfields of the towering Himalayas.

His views on Bigfoot, however, are entirely different. "I am convinced that Bigfoot exists," he states. He then adds that there has to be something in northwest America that leaves manlike footprints, and those footprints need some explaining.

It's the size of the tracks that intrigues Dr. Napier more than anything else. He believes that the creature who made the tracks must be at least eight feet tall and weigh upward of eight hundred pounds. The idea of such huge creatures stomping barefoot through the forests of northwest America is hard to believe, he admits, then goes on to say that the evidence of footprints and eyewitness accounts forces him to believe that these creatures do exist. Hairy giants *are* roaming around in the United States and Canada. Not everyone believes this, of course, but that's not important. The fact that a growing number of scientists are now taking Bigfoot seriously is of far greater importance.

The question that puzzles both scientists and laymen the most is this one: Just what in the world is Bigfoot, anyway? Is he an ape or a human? Or is he an apelike human or a humanlike ape? Everyone agrees that he came here from Asia, but no one knows exactly what he is.

Scientists are naturally very reluctant to go out on a limb. Because of Bigfoot's enormous size, Ivan Sanderson cautiously suggests that he might be a humanoid—a creature somewhere between man and what we call an animal. The remains of gigantic eight- to twelve-foot-tall humanlike apes called *Gigantopithecus* have been unearthed in Asia. It's possible then, Sanderson says, that some of these creatures could have survived, crossed the land bridge between Asia and North America, and settled down comfortably in their new home.

John Green, the noted Canadian authority on the

sasquatch, tends to agree with Sanderson. He claims that the sasquatches are not human or near-human. Their size, hairiness, and bulkiness go beyond human limitations and they show no sign of human mental ability. Green believes that they have survived through the ages because of their superb physical equipment and not because of their brains. He's not saying, of course, that Bigfoot is a great big brainless dummy. He's simply saying that he's not too smart. Like Sanderson, Green feels that the sasquatch is probably a direct descendant of *Gigantopithecus* but differs from other apes in various ways.

Dr. John Napier states that the Java Man and the Neanderthal Man are "custom-built suspects for the American Bigfoot." He hastily adds, however, that this suspicion is a very long shot indeed and terribly unscientific. Both the Java Man and Neanderthal Man made crude tools and knew how to build fires, cook their food, and cover themselves with skins.

Poor old not-too-bright Bigfoot doesn't know how to do any of these things. He runs around as naked as the day he was born and he knows nothing at all about fire or tools. Dr. Napier hints that Bigfoot might possibly be a descendant of man, but can't believe that the big fellow could have gone so completely to pieces over the ages. Surely the knowledge possessed by his ancestors would have been passed down from father to son.

Dr. Napier is too cautious to make any definite statements and he certainly won't make any until he meets Bigfoot face-to-face. The fact that he has publicly declared that he believes in the existence of Bigfoot should be good enough for all of us.

Whether Bigfoot is an ape or a man, an apelike man or a manlike ape isn't really important to most people.

The important thing is that there's a curious, shy, elusive, hair-covered giant roaming around in our mountains and forests today. The biggest ones may be more than ten feet tall and weigh over one thousand pounds. Although they're enormously powerful, they seem to be far more curious than dangerous. People who live in areas where Bigfoot is frequently seen are very fond of their hairy monster and wish him the very best of luck.

Little Jacko, you'll remember, was captured by a train crew near Yale, British Columbia, in 1882. Roger Patterson shot his remarkable film in 1967. This proves that Bigfoot can be photographed as well as captured. If one of the creatures doesn't walk into Ron Olson's trap soon, then further action should be taken.

After seeing Patterson's movie, Dr. Osman Hill suggested that a truly scientific expedition should go into Bigfoot country and find out just exactly what these giant creatures are. Americans have sent men to the moon, and we now know that it's not made of cheese. So wouldn't it be nice if we knew who or what the monsters are that live practically in our own backyards?

Meanwhile, it's fun to know that the age of giants still isn't over and that the mystery surrounding them may soon be solved.

Everyone likes giants and we'd all like to know a little bit more about those living right here in North America.

SUGGESTIONS FOR FURTHER READING

BOOKS

Green, John. *On the Track of the Sasquatch*. Agassiz, British Columbia: Cheam Publishing, 1968.

———. *The Sasquatch File*. Agassiz, British Columbia: Cheam Publishing, 1973.

———. *Year of the Sasquatch*. Agassiz, British Columbia: Cheam Publishing, 1970.

Heuvelmans, Bernard. *On the Trail of Unknown Animals*. New York: Hill and Wang, 1965.

Napier, John. *Bigfoot: The Yeti and Sasquatch in Myth and Reality*. New York: E. P. Dutton & Company, 1973.

Patterson, Roger. *Do Abominable Snowmen of America Really Exist?* Yakima: Northwest Research Association, 1966.

Roosevelt, Theodore. *Wilderness Hunter*. New York: G. P. Putnam's Sons, 1893.

Sanderson, Ivan. *Abominable Snowmen: Legend Come to Life*. Philadelphia: Chilton Book Company, 1973.

Tchernine, Odette. *In Pursuit of the Abominable Snowman*. New York: Taplinger Publishing Company, 1971.

PERIODICALS

Hansen, Frank. "I Killed the Ape-Man Creature of Whiteface." Saga (July 1970).

Harrison, George, "On the Track of Bigfoot." *National Wildlife* (October/November 1970).

Kirkpatrick, Dick. "The Search for Bigfoot." *National Wildlife* (April/May 1968).

Masters, John. "The Abominable Snowman." *Harper's* (January 1959).

Moore, G. "I Met the Abominable Snowman." *Sports Afield* (May 1957).

Ortner, Everett. "Do 'Extinct' Animals Still Survive?" *Popular Science Monthly* (April 1969).

Sanderson, Ivan. "The Abominable Snowman." *True* (May 1950).

——. "The Strange Story of America's Abominable Snowman." *True* (December 1959).

——. "A New Look at America's Mystery Giant." *True* (March 1960).

——. "Abominable Snowmen Are Here!" *True* (April 1961).

——. "California's Abominable Snowman." *Argosy* (February 1968).

——. "Wisconsin's Abominable Snowman." *Argosy* (April 1969).

——. "The Missing Link." *Argosy* (May 1969).

Soule, Garner. "The World's Most Mysterious Footprints." *Popular Science* (December 1952).

INDEX

ABOUT THE AUTHOR

Elwood D. Baumann was born in Saskatchewan, Canada, and is a graduate of the University of Wisconsin. After many years as a teacher and principal in schools in Venezuela and eastern Turkey, he took up writing as a vocation and travel as an avocation and has now been in one hundred and five countries on six continents.

Mr. Baumann first became interested in Abominable Snowmen while living in Nepal. He had numerous discussions on the subject with many Nepalis, Tibetan refugees, and British mountaineers. It wasn't until some years later that he first learned about Abominable Snowmen in our own country. His interest in the creatures led him to the Pacific Northwest where he spent many months interviewing eyewitnesses and Bigfoot researchers. Although he has not personally made Bigfoot's acquaintance, Mr. Baumann's experiences in the course of writing this book have made him a Bigfoot believer and he is an enthusiastic member of the North American Wildlife Research Association.

Elwood Baumann is the author of *The Loch Ness Monster*.

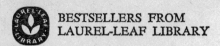

BESTSELLERS FROM LAUREL-LEAF LIBRARY

"IT RAN UPRIGHT LIKE A MAN, BUT I DON'T THINK IT WAS HUMAN . . . IT WAS ALL COVERED WITH HAIR, IT HAD LONG SWINGING ARMS, AND IT LOOKED LIKE IT WAS EIGHT OR TEN FEET TALL!"

In 1958, a road-building crew in the wilderness area of Humboldt County, California was terrorized by a huge, hairy, manlike giant that left enormous footprints and carried off equipment no human could possibly lift. Stories appeared in local newspapers, *The New York Times* picked up the account, and Bigfoot was introduced to the world.

ELWOOD D. BAUMANN, foremost investigator of the Loch Ness Monster and Nepal's Abominable Snowman, has chronicled dozens of strange and exciting stories of Bigfoot, those who have met him, and those who hope to. Here are drawings, photographs, and a clip from the famous 16 mm movie film showing an actual Bigfoot in the forest.

BIGFOOT EXISTS!

THE LAUREL-LEAF LIBRARY brings together under a single imprint outstanding works of fiction and nonfiction particularly suitable for young adult readers, both in and out of the classroom. The series is under the editorship of Charles F. Reasoner, Professor of Elementary Education, New York University, and Carolyn W. Carmichael, Associate Professor, Department of Communication Sciences, Kean College of New Jersey.